D1249268

FoR BERYL...

Lugworm Island Hopping

with every good
wish.

from 'LVGWoRm"
Brenda
and
Ken
X X r

Lugworm Island Hopping

KEN DUXBURY

With drawings, maps and photographs
by the author

Pelham Books

First published in Great Britain by Pelham Books Ltd
52 Bedford Square, London WC1B 3EF
1976

ISBN 0 7207 0940 7

Printed in Great Britain by
Tonbridge Printers Ltd, Peach Hall Works, Tonbridge, Kent
in Garamond eleven on twelve point on paper supplied by
P. F. Bingham Ltd, and bound by James Burn
at Esher, Surrey

To

JOHN

who lent me his
house on Ensay

Contents

Illustrations

Maps

Cornish Wind

Unfettered, free, an ocean's breath
— you come,
Knife-edged laughing Cornish wind,
You shock the cold dew-misted land to life
Flinging a spray of screaming gulls
high on the cliffs

And we, poor earthbound mortals, stand
with feet of clay.
Reading your message in the waves . . .
I went that way . . .
. . . that way . . .

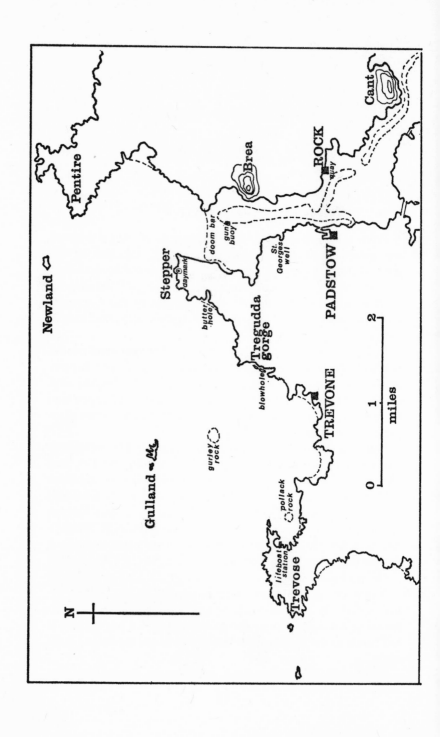

Chapter One

The Eye of the Wind

Thank God for that west wind!

From a thousand miles of ocean, pure as an Angel's breath she comes, gusting free until ... WHAM! Baulked by the great cliffs of Cornwall, she bowls keel-over-truck. And here are we, ripping our spinnakers in greeting and drawing in great lungfulls of virgin air – with the rest of the Continent down to leeward getting all our stale vapours, and good luck to them!

Make no mistake, it's a good place to live, out west on the northern shore of this rugged peninsula, and if you happen to own a dinghy – a dinghy as fine and noble-hearted and adventurous as the immortal *Lugworm* – and you happen also to be potty about islands, why, I tell you there's no better place to be on this earth!

Not that we're overbestowed with islands. The nearest to this Camel Estuary where *Lugworm* lives is the Scillies, and they're forty-five horrendous miles down this iron-bound coast to the Land's End. After that you've still got another twenty-two miles of heaving ocean past the bones of *Torrey Canyon* on the Seven Stones reef before the daymark on St Martin's Isle beckons you in to safety ... and it's no place to be in a dinghy unless you're tired of life ...

Or in *Lugworm*.

'Come on,' I said to my wife B. the spring after *Lugworm* had sailed the two of us back from Greece, 'the disease is breaking out again. Shove the toothbrushes in a bag and we'll sail down to the Scillies for a month just to get the feel of it all again.'

'Uh ... uh,' she commented, nibbling the Ryvita. She was

11

looking at me hard and I knew immediately it was a tactical error to have broached the thought at breakfast. I ought to have learned from experience and waited at least until lunch-time.

'We've already done over three and a half thousand miles bouncing about on the seas – and *Lugworm*'s tent is getting leaky. For glory's sake, haven't you had enough yet?' And she nibbled on, deeply disturbed.

Of course, you've got to know B. to understand what I mean by that. It isn't that she's not besotted with *Lugworm* and wouldn't hesitate to ruin her best bodice under the bilges scraping off the barnacles but . . . it's a sort of 'love-hate' relationship she has with the sea. 'It's caused me more sheer torment than anything else in my life,' she'll state. 'More plain discomfort, more wet, bruised, downright misery than any girl has a right to expect.' And of course, she's right.

But as every sailor knows : that has nothing whatever to do with it. All such things pretty soon get lost in the rich tapestry of memories that gild even the most frightful event with a golden halo of remembering.

There was that pre-B. day on the Doom Bar, for instance, back in 1957. Every besodden second of it glows as brightly now as it did eighteen years ago. I see it all again, the sweep of the blue summer sea out there to the north beyond Newland Rock, and a raven-haired girl called Jo with me in a boat even smaller than *Lugworm*, looking out past the sandy beaches under the golf links. Three frustrated hours we'd spent towing a maggot hopefully up and down that stretch between the bar and Rock quay with neither bite nor jiggle to raise a hope, and we both felt there were better things to be doing.

Then I caught Jo's eyes wandering seaward toward New-land. 'Wouldn't it be more fun if we went out there to the island?' she whispered. 'I mean, we might catch a mackerel or two outside the bar, it's so lovely and calm . . . and there are so many people in here . . .'

I knew what she meant.

But I was older than she, and responsible to boot. I had to put up a resistance. 'Not likely. Not over that bar.'

'The tide's rising,' she answered, quietly.

I looked again at the bar. Not a whimper of surf was there,

and she was quite right, the tide was rising. We were getting into deeper water with every minute! But I knew that bar backwards ... knew it was just when you felt certain that the danger was over, just when you were balanced in innocence halfway over that sandbank stretching across the estuary mouth that Neptune would heave up a drencher. And a drencher in a fourteen-foot sailing dinghy is more than enough.

'Nothing doing!' I stuck to my guns and we stooged back again past Ship-my-Pumps point. She fretted. On the next leg toward the entrance it started again.

'Wouldn't it be grand to disappear behind that rock out there ... I've never been out in the real sea in a small boat before ... couldn't we just ... ?'

Now I had been watching the bar like a hawk since she first voiced the idea. Not a heave, nor whimper nor fret of white had there been this last hour, and with the rising tide the estuary was becoming more crowded: there was at least one other boat plugging up and down getting in the way of our lines. I had been over the bar often before in that dinghy, but I knew there was some heavy weather frolicking about out there to the westward, and sooner or later that meant there would be a swell running up the Bristol Channel. Still, as I say, there was no sign of it that morning; even the gulls were snoozing, so soporific was the heat and the peace.

'Put on that lifejacket,' I ordered. Remember this was in pre-marital days and I had an image to keep up. Rugged responsibility if I remember rightly. Her eyes flashed.

'Oooo ... Ken. Are we really going ... ?'

'The lifejacket,' I repeated. 'And blow it up.'

There was a sweet zephyr of a south wind and we ran up goosewinged past St George's Well close to the western shore, then struck out to the centre of the channel, leaving Gun buoy to port as we ghosted on toward Stepper point. Neptune acknowledged our presence with a gentle sigh as our shadow slid over the sand of the bar a few feet below, and seaward the world was bright and blue, full of hope and mackerel and ...

I saw it coming.

Halfway in innocence isn't really honest: I was halfway in experience, but could do nothing to stop that swell advanc-

13

ing. Round the point of Stepper and across the broad mouth of the estuary it stretched, the ghastly smooth ridge of a silent, menacing mountain.

We watched it undulating toward us, pregnant with intent, rearing up inexorably as it began to feel the shallowing seabed . . . and the hair on the nape of my neck wriggled.

'Jo,' I croaked, 'whatever happens, HANG ON TO THE BOAT – DON'T GET SWEPT OFF!' I'll never know whether she had an inkling at that moment what I was talking about, but it's certain she did seconds later. That great mountain of swell reared up, glared us in the eye, curled over with a fiendish grin not twenty feet away and plunged down its own face with a roar fit to split your eardrums.

'Hold on!' I shrieked as the wall of foam hit our bows, and I have a lifelong recollection of the boat's stem swinging vertically above us, her stern plunging down into a white cauldron of threshing water and then . . . a green silent world of bubbles. Something hit me in the teeth. I think it was the rudder which had come unshipped in the maelstrom – and then I was gasping for air and clawing at the half-submerged bottom of the boat which had turned turtle, pitchpoled backwards, and there was Jo, bobbing about like an orange cork, enmeshed in a tangle of rigging and sails, all aspluther with foam. I looked frantically seaward: another like that and the two of us would be needing gills! There was another, but, Neptune be praised, not quite like that. It rose, teetered, and then changed its mind. We rose with it, balanced for a hideous moment on its knife-edge, and then slid down its back as it rolled on inexorably to lose its energy farther up the estuary without actually breaking.

Half an hour later the flood tide had drifted us and the mangled dinghy into water shallow enough for us to get a foot on the bottom, and then we pulled the boat on to the beach and sorted out the mess. As we were collecting all the bits and pieces together, oars, sails, bottom boards and our loose gear, down comes the lifeboat tender fairly bristling with Padstow fishermen – and I got the telling off I shall remember all my life, and fully deserved!

But why am I telling you all this, it's nothing to do with *Lugworm*, still less with B. It's just that I remember it so well

14

... only now, as I have said, the event has a rosy halo of romance about it which was lacking at the time.

Where was I?

Islands. No: B. didn't take the bait as I hoped she might, but in the end we hit on a compromise. 'You sail down there,' she said, 'and after I've thinned out the lettuces I'll fly over and join you for a week or so ... but I shall have to get back to pick the beans!' So that was it. Just *Lugworm* and me.

It could be worse.

Now I must tell you, because it is pertinent to the adventures which follow, that the previous winter I had built a garage. Resulting from this I had fifteen thin bendy deal planks left over – offcuts from the rafters – which I had to pay for, and what else can you do with fifteen wafer-thin planks save break two of them, swear, and build a skiff dinghy with the remaining thirteen lucky ones?

So *Ben Gunn* was born, light as a feather, skinned with an old bedsheet and painted white to keep the water out. I tow her behind *Lugworm* and she rides the seas like a mermaid, albeit in a permanent quandary regarding her sex. Nine feet in length and three feet in the beam she is, and just for good measure I carved a hideous face on the bow with a black eyepatch, and brought the painter out through piratical teeth just to make *Lugworm* go that bit faster, being permanently chased as it were. Why call her *Ben Gunn*? I can't remember, but it seemed appropriate at the time.

That spring morning Phoebus was virile with glory. I'd launched *Lugworm* and *Ben* the previous day and spent the night aboard up the estuary hidden in behind Cant Creek to sort myself out after the chaos of a winter ashore. There are a thousand little things you forget about living under a tent in a dinghy: long since, for instance, both B. and I had given up the idea of airbeds. No matter what quality they are, after a week or so of squashing in between the knees of the centre-plate casing and the side of the boat, they develop a death rattle. You spend half the sleeping hours giving the kiss of life and for all the good it does you might as well save your breath and go to sleep. Far better to spread out the spare sails,

15

jerseys, towels and whatever ... anything that will separate your haunches from the ribbed bottomboards ... and you sleep like a log!

Lugworm's main mast pivots at deck level. It's only a moment's work to unship the mizzen then hinge back the foremast, remove the hinge bolt and support the whole mast complete with gaff and sail still lashed thereto, on crutches to form a stout ridgepole. A white waterproof pvc tent then ships over this and laps outside the gunwales for the entire length of the boat, securing with short tie-lines to a strong rope girdle with which one encircles the hull. The after-end of the tent has flaps, and depending on the weather the tent can be rolled forward to expose any amount of the afterdeck you require – it's remarkably convenient and has the added advantage that when at anchor the boat naturally faces into the wind, so any rain sweeps back and away from the open end. *Lugworm* is one of the original wooden eighteen-foot Drascombe Luggers, and the design very cleverly ensures that any water slopping on to the sterndeck flows aft to disappear down the outboard 'well', which is inside the transom. Two lockers stretch back under this sterndeck, one either side of the rudder casing, and we use one for food and the other for the petrol feed tank and spare chandlery. Clothes and bedding go in another capacious locker under the foredeck, while odds and sods like hairbrushes and charts and bars of chocolate stow up in elastic-fronted netting beneath the two sidedecks. It's all very shipshape, and you always know where everything is – either somewhere in the boat, or gone for good!

I'd kissed B. goodbye the evening before. 'If the weather heard the shipping forecast, I'll be off before high water early tomorrow and catching the first of the ebb from Trevose to help me down to St Ives,' I told her.

Do you know this north coast of Cornwall? From the Rock Estuary to Land's End it's just as God left it when things cooled down ... rugged offlying islets – not really islands – more like headlands that have fallen off and then changed their minds. Cliffs: you'll not better them this side of the Hebrides and in between lie those glorious and often inaccessible sweeps of strand. It's a lotus eater's paradise when the sun shines – and enough to curdle the blood when the

16

"LUGWORM"

©KEN DUXBURY

Length: 18 ft.

Beam: 6 ft. 3 in.

Draught (plate up): 10 in.
(plate down): 3 ft. 6 in.

Total weight (approx.): 1,000 lb.

Total sail area: 130 sq. ft.

Rig: Gunter Yawl

Outboard: Mercury 4 hp. longshaft

Centreplate: Half-inch steel. 120 lb.

Rudder: Quarter-inch steel: 29 lb.

Construction: Thames Marine plywood

storms come.

Now it's thirty-two miles to St Ives from Stepper Point and there's only Newquay in between. Both these ports spell disaster in a dinghy if a northerly swell starts running, for the surf breaks well off the harbour entrances at low water springs.

'Remember I love you, and take care of *Lugworm*,' B. had said as she blew a kiss from the Rock wall . . . and here I was, off.

Off!

Is there ANYTHING to equal that first chuckle of water under your hull at the start of a new summer cruise? The thrill of response as the boat heels under the press of her sails, free as the wind itself . . . and all the cares and tribulations of life ashore falling away like nightmares from a waking man!

Glory, but what a morning that was!

The flanks of the estuary were brilliant with sand glowing in the first shafts of the rising sun. Behind them to eastward rolled the washed green of the golf links, and beyond that the balding head of Brea hill folded the colours gently back and up into that pure unbroken blue of a Cornish spring sky. I could smell the young gorse as I beat out against a light northerly, tacking close under the old quarry south of Stepper, and *Lugworm*'s wake gurgled and rippled a paean of happiness astern. Before we were over the bar I was stripped to the minimals and awakening again to that delicious tingle of sun and wind and spray on my skin . . . looking to all the days ahead . . . endless days of freedom . . . with summer just over the horizon!

'Nobody,' I bellowed to *Lugworm*, 'nobody has any right to be as happy as this!' And she dipped, and shook her mizzen, and laughed with me, for she, too, was feeling the roll of deep blue water again, and had caught a first sight of that incomparable sweep of coast down to Trevose, with Gulland and Newland set like emeralds in the amethyst sea.

We freed off to the west close under the daymark on Stepper, reached down past Butter Hole and headed for the blowhole at Tregudda Gorge, that great buttress of cliffs which has cracked off close north of Trevone. It was here I mined my first amethysts for an ill-fated engagement ring for Jo, and since you've been introduced you might as well know what befell.

You can get down to sea-level from the land at Tregudda Gorge, provided you're lithe as a mountain goat, young, and mad. As I say, it was for Jo I did it, before pitch-poling on the bar. We used to go courting out there on the clifftops, backalong, and I knew from past experience that at low tide springs it was possible to cross the bottom of the gorge by leaping from rock to slippery rock until you clambered on to the base of that vast chunk that has cracked away. There is a vein of quartz there, and if you are lucky you can find a bit of it that's beginning to turn blue. I called it amethyst, and Jo believed me.

'What's your favourite stone?' I asked her about a month after we met, and to show which way the wind was blowing. 'Amethyst,' she said, and that was that. Why fossick about with jewellers when you can mine the things all a-virgin on your own doorstep? So there we were one sultry noon at dead low water springs with a coil of spare halyard and a hammer atop the cliffs looking down into the gorge.

'Sure you want to come down with me?' I asked her.

'As long as you hold tight to the other end of that rope,' she replied, taking a cautious look over the near vertical cliff. So together we went to where a peculiar natural slope leads halfway down the cliff face, like a ship's gangway without any steps. After that – about sixty feet down – things get a bit difficult. There are places to get a hold of, and cracks to jam a foot in, but you have to look hard for them!

It was fine to start with. Jo went first, a bowline hitched under her bosom, and I stayed a bit behind jammed firmly and keeping the rope taut so that in the event of mishaps there would be no disastrous jerks. But by the time we reached the end of the slope, Jo had got the wobbles. There was still a long way to go and the swell was booming into a gulley vertically beneath with terrifying power, launching a shower of rainbows just to leeward. It was fun.

'Sure you want to come on?' I asked.

'Expect it'll be all right after this bit,' she answered, glancing apprehensively back from where we'd come. But of course it wasn't. Things got progressively worse and it developed into one of those classic situations where the lesser of two evils is undoubtedly to go on straight into the jaws of Hell! Before we were near sea-level, Jo was a lump of raven-haired jelly.

'There must be some other way out of this,' she squawked above the roar, quivering on a ledge just out of the sea's reach. Along the narrow crack of the gorge the dark sea heaved and fell in predatory surges like some slow-breathing monster. Close under us the swell crashed in to send a million frustrated spouts cascading up the cliff face. The water close aboard was turned into soapsuds and everything was echoing damp.

'No,' I shouted. 'Tell you what . . . you stay right here and I'll go on across the gorge for the amethysts. Don't worry, we'll work our way back up in our own time . . . won't take long . . . the tide's turning anyway so I must be quick . . . just stay there darling.' I blew her a kiss and inched along the rocks to where the gorge was narrower. Farther in I could see the smooth rounded top of a boulder which broke surface occasionally some halfway across the gully. Two good leaps and a bit of luck, and that islet was mine for the mining. I got to a point from which I could lunge out and down on to the boulder, waited for the sea to breathe out again . . . and leapt.

It was like Yul Brynner's scalp with butter on it, that boulder! Perhaps I landed on it but I remember nothing save the sudden cold of the water beyond, and marvelling how deep it was so near to the cliff face. In I went, to the crown of my head, but I was wearing only the hammer so there wasn't much to worry about and being totally immersed it seemed just as sensible to carry on over as come back. By the time I'd swum to a convenient ledge the sea was breathing in again – up I was lifted, graceful as a bird – and seconds later the water was cascading from all around leaving me and the hammer high if not dry, scrabbling across the barnacles clear of the next surge. I looked back for Jo to give her a comforting wave, but the haunch of the islet hid her, and there was no time to waste.

I know that climb well. The southern flank of the islet rises in a sixty degree slope, then breaks into crags and crevasses higher up. The top of the slope is yellow with flashing quartz crystals – maybe it was the original fault line which broke away from the land, for the vein is quite exposed and, as I have said, if you search, there are pockets where the crystals turn mauve and bluish. If you search.

I searched. They're not two-a-penny those pockets, but I found one at last about halfway up and battered it to a powder trying to remove one tiny piece that might look like an amethyst. So I went up higher and found another in a small crack. Time stood still as I worked at that cavity. I hacked all around it, breaking away the incredibly hard rock and working in behind to prize off just one piece in a solid chunk, and eventually it gave in. I had a piece big as half a brick and it looked just like Jo's eyes. In a paroxyism of passion I scrambled up to the very top of the islet, lay full length and peered over the precipitous northern face. Down there, maybe a hundred and fifty feet below, a tiny figure was crouched against the cliff face. She looked oddly damp and paralysed. I waved and shouted but the booming seas below drowned my voice and anyway the dear girl was so short-sighted I doubt she could see the islet, never mind this palpi-tating dot on top. So I piled a few more chunks of stone on to the cairn I'd built there the summer before, just for good measure, and started back down, clutching the precious jewels.

Of course, the sea hadn't waited. In fact as I took stock of the situation it was evident that it had risen a few feet since my moist crossing, and really you'd be surprised what a differ-ence a few feet can make. Asleep and heaving peacefully it had been when I floundered over, but now it was wide awake and yawning with breakers crashing into both ends of the gorge. Yul Brynner had sunk and every minute things were getting worse. Suddenly I felt cold.

There was now one place only to land on the cliff-face opposite – a narrow ledge that afforded handholds from which one might reach up and grasp a crack above it. From there, with luck, I could inch along hand-over-hand until my feet came within reach of a shelf. There was nothing else for it: clutching the hammer and stones in my left hand, I jumped.

Have you ever tried swimming with a hammer and a brick? They don't help. Lopsidedly I clawed across to the ledge and waited for a sea to lift me up. At the critical moment I grabbed the wet ledge, dropped the hammer, lost my hold and crashed back into that perishing dark water, shuddering now with the cold, but still clutching those precious stones. There seemed little else for it but to swim right along the gully toward Jo, hoping to gain a footing on the way. Halfway along I clambered out, teeth chattering, to claw and slither slowly under the cliff face . . . in a world that had suddenly grown twice as big, four times as cold, dark echoing and noisy to boot. But, at last, there was Jo, cowering exactly where I'd left her, drenched through from the spray and crying.

'Darling,' I gasped, appearing over the top of a slimy boulder . . . 'I've got them, they're beauti . . .'

'Ah!' she jumped, 'Oh . . . you . . . YOU WRETCH . . . you . . .' She was sobbing and spitting with venom all in one. I'd never before seen a woman really angry and scared stiff at the same time, and it was puzzling.

'You FIEND!' she sobbed. 'You've been hours. I'm drenched, and cold, and miserable, and frightened to death. I hate you . . . I thought you'd drowned . . . oh . . . JUST GET ME OUT OF THIS HELLISH PLACE!'

I showed her the stones.

'Oh, DAMN THE QUARTZ,' she croaked. Just get me out of here. It's all right for you – you're a man,' and she glared at me hard before adding, 'and an exhibitionist at that!'

So I got dressed and together we clambered somehow back up that cliff face, but we were both pretty depressed 'ere we regained the top. No, the amethysts were not a success. I can't remember which disintegrated first, the jewels or the engagement – but it was the bar that finished it all.

Never mind, I was coming up to that blowhole. It works only when the tide is at a critical level, and only then when a long swell comes running in from the north-west. Then Tregudda takes a really mighty breath – and bellows! It's awesome and deafening to watch. There's a subterranean cavern underneath amethyst islet whose entrance, on the seaward face, is just high enough to clear sea level at half tide. As is usually the case with these blowholes, the cave expands into a sizeable cavern inside, and at a certain sea level the air gets trapped as a heaving great swell rolls into the entrance – and you can guess what happens then. The pressure is enormous: all the power in that swell, baulked by the cliff, compresses the

Tregudda Gorge

air inside the cavern and out it comes through the very top of the entrance with a blast like a hurricane. It roars as it comes, a deep sonorous organ note like the explosion of the foghorn on Trevose Head, and it squirts a geyser of water out with it for good measure! I tell you, it turns you into a jelly to get near when it's really enjoying itself, and the spume goes flying up the cliff face like some primaeval sea-monster's breath. Then it hisses and gurgles as the swell retreats and the air is sucked in again ready for the next performance. No place to be in *Lugworm* when that little frolic is on, I can tell you. But this day, as *Lugworm, Ben* and I headed down the coast, all was quiet – indeed the top of the cave was well beneath sea-level, being high water springs, so we just blew it a kiss and checked that the stone cairn was still up there atop the islet, and thought a bit about ravenhead . . .

So we reached down toward Trevone. But something was wrong with the weather. From a nice northerly that would have made bliss of a broad reach right down the coast, the wind had fallen away, dithered about a bit and set in a drift from the west, with little more than a sniff of north in it, if that. The sky, moreover, beyond the horizon to the westward looked like most westerly skies hereabouts – frontal and rain-laden. My heart sank. *Lugworm*, bless her, isn't the best of craft when working up to windward. She's built for sea-worthiness and it's asking too much of her buxom shape and rig to expect her to cover much ground on a dead beat. The sensible thing was to anchor under the lifeboat station north of Trevose Head and wait.

Now, I must tell you that the tidal stream, close inshore between Stepper Point and Trevose Head, does peculiar things. It swirls round in a vast circle, the north-eastgoing stream begins by running northward, then swings east-north-east and finishes in an easterly direction at a rate of about one knot springs and half a knot neaps. The south-west stream starts roughly in that direction, then swings round toward the north-west, its greatest rate being attained when it's running south-west. I had counted on gaining the advantage of that westerly stream, but, as is so often the case when rock-hopping within yards of the shore, found a contrary flow which, coupled with the now adverse wind, left *Lugworm* stooging about off Trevone with nothing save a raging appetite to goad her on to an anchorage . . . so I brought her alloy topsail into use and chugged at a steady four knots under the Mercury outboard, skirting south of Pollack rock (which is a thing I'd never do when there is much swell running) and brought up close under the new lifeboat slip.

It's a grand anchorage this. The prevailing south-westerlies can ramp and roar and churn the seas into frothy pea-soup, but you're O.K. snugged under the high ground to weather. Provided you're well clear of the launching slipway, all is well, but mark that: for when that lifeboat rattles down the slip it stops for nothing and the bow wave alone is enough to capsize a tiddler if she's too close. At anything but highest of springs there's a sweet little beach at the foot of the cliffs where one can while away pleasant hours sunbathing with a maid. Mind you, it's no place to be caught when the wind turns east!

On this occasion, however, something alien was in the air. At first I couldn't make out quite what was afoot, but gradually I located the seat of it. The seabirds which normally nest on the offlying rocks just north of the slipway were whirling in a cacophony of distress. Now this, while to be expected if one starts clambering about the rocks, is most unusual when you're half a mile off. Something was wrong, and I was examining the area through the glasses when I first caught a whiff of the trouble . . . a faint but horrifying smell of corpse. This, coupled with the activity of the birds, was puzzling, for the air hereabouts is sweet as nectar. No sooner had I dropped anchor just clear of the lifeboat buoy, than *Ben* was alongside and taking me over to the tip of beach which was showing with the first of the ebb. You can't flirt with rocks in *Ben* – one glance from a barnacle and she's sunk – but I gave her a stout protective wooden strip of keel that allows her to be dragged up beaches – provided she's held level.

So off to that craggy outcrop I hied, agog with curiosity, and swam across the insulating gully of water which makes it such a favourite breeding ground for the herring gulls, being out of reach of marauders generally. But I could wish I had not. No sooner was I climbing the fifty-foot crags than tragedy declared itself. Newborn chicks and mottled youngsters just

25

ready to take wing were lying dead by the score, evidently rotting a week or so, for the stink was unbearable . . . and out in the bay the parent birds continued to set up a dismal wail of alarm and despair. To this day I don't know the cause: rogue black-backs possibly, but unlikely in such wanton massacre proportions. Man more likely, but pollution most probably, for none of the chicks appeared to be mutilated. Anyway, I collected as many as I could reach and threw them into the sea to reduce the smell, but the event cast a sad air of gloom over the day, and I was glad to get back up to weather in *Lugworm* and rig the tent, for the sky was turning grey.

With the ageing day came rain, and a freshening westerly. It drummed on the tent like a machine-gun, and *Lugworm*, caught by the swirls of wind bowling over the cliffs, chuckled as she ranged about, until I lowered the heavy metal centre-plate which kept her steady and more or less head-to-wind. It's good to be inside her in this sort of weather. With the stern flaps wide open she remains quite dry under the tent, for as I have said the wind and rain sweeps past no matter from what direction, for the boat always lies bow-to-wind. You can sit for hours just watching the changing scene as she slowly describes an arc, bringing now this, now that bit of coast or sea within view. Come darkness, you light the candle and brew up some supper on the small camping stove, then wash it down with a strong coffee laced with a tot of something to keep the warmth in . . . and there's the stars, and perhaps the moon, sweeping across your real live cinema screen out of the stern.

But I remember as that afternoon wore on the rain increased and a dismal swell started rolling into the bay, residue of the previous day's northerly wind, and since I was anchored in little more than six feet of water at low tide it was feeling the bottom and throwing *Lugworm* about quite a bit. I don't mind this all that much, considering it better than being farther out where there was somewhat less swell but a deal more wind and sea . . . so there I was, listening to the rain, curled up in my sleeping bag and *Ben* sinking fast under the deluge, when disaster smote. I'd set off without my hairbrush! I'd also left behind a spare can of petrol, a tin-opener, and my metric chart of the Scillies, but these were minor details ... the hairbrush brought me up all standing. An itchy scalp is one thing I can't stand before breakfast and I've got one of those splendid rubber padded things with bristles like steel: the day begins with it. Truly it was a disaster.

Ashore, the swell was now booming against the cliffs just south of the slipway and the surf around the bay eastward was fit to turn a sailor into a bath attendant: no place to land in *Ben Gunn*, and lifeboat beach is inaccessible save from seaward, so telegrams were out of the question. I'd sunk into one of those blank states of mental absence which only real sailors can achieve hour after hour with the boat all but standing on her head when a deep-throated roar penetrated the gloom. Squinting through the tent flap I saw the fangs of a high-powered cruiser bearing down on me. It drew abreast, throttled back, and started a hideous *pas de deux* with *Lugworm*.

'What the hell are YOU doing here – trouble?' came the hail. It was friends.

'You bet,' I roared back at them. 'I'm outward bound for the Scillies, but I've forgotten my hairbrush. Tell B.' They looked at me as though I were some sort of phenomenon, then throttled up and flew off into the pall. Fine friends!

Next dawn found me just lying there itching and listening to the thunder of rain when ... that familiar roar hove up again. A heavy object skeetered into the tent and the roar was just an echo before I'd split my sleeping bag. I picked up the parcel. Inside was a tin of beans and my hairbrush. That's what I call friends! There were also five separate letters from B. all in capitals: I D I O T. On the back was a big cross which made me feel much better.

The tide was ebbing, the rain had stopped, and since my scalp had stopped itching there was nothing to prevent *Lugworm* spreading her wings again ... except a total absence of wind. So I stepped her masts, set the mizzen to help digestion and lowered the outboard. Together we puttered off westward with *Ben* in tow.

If you don't stop to pick winkles you can just about fetch St Ives from Trevose on a fully stretched ebb. But my scalp

... The boat all but standing on her head

had accounted for nearly an hour of that tide, and when a brisk westerly began to draw breath we still had some twelve miles to go, and the seas were wearing that certain look.

'It's Godrevy or bust!' I encouraged *Lugworm*, thinking we could gain a lee under the islet on which the lighthouse stands, for we could make it out some eight miles ahead. With the wind bang on the nose I knew it was engine or nothing, but set all sail just to help – which is why, I suppose, after a sniff or two the blessed engine stopped. Dead cut and not a spark of life. We eased off a point to make the sails do all the work and first tack brought us up under the ruin of Wheal Coates Mine, Chapel Porth. We put about, and there we were all set back to Wales! Meanwhile the sea was, well, like any sea that's rubbing the wind up the wrong way: bouncy and wet. It was raining again, too, and morale was falling for I knew that before Godrevy we'd be bashing both wind and tide under sail alone – and there was no future in that. The alternative was a dismal run back to Newquay ten miles astern. Determinedly we put in a few wet tacks, close under the towering cliffs, and found ourselves looking at Portreath.

Now Portreath is a place I've never before in my life so

Above, author . . . and crew; *below,* Sennen Cove — no place
to be in a northerly! *Lugworm,* with tent rigged, drawn up on
the slipway

Top, St. Mary's harbour, with French barquentine and baggywrinkle galore; *centre, left,* Alphonse in *Ben Gunn; right,* '... even caught a thumping great pollack'; *bottom,* Hottentot Bay; Great Arthur isle with Nornour in the middle background and St. Martin's on left

much as noticed. On my chart it's not marked as a harbour, so it's had scant attention on previous passages down this coast. But under the circumstances we were foraging about with greater interest than usual on shore: and there under the foot of a horrifying black cliff poked the end of a tiny stone mole! Moles generally mean holes, and any hole was acceptable rather than regurgitating all those hard-gained miles ... so in we went, hell-for-leather on starboard, and freed off wonderfully just to make a show.

There were some dedicated fishermen on the end of the mole, and – have you noticed? – it's an odd thing, but shoreside fisherfolk seem to think that boats which come in from sea are ethereal things with no substance whatever ... gossamer visions that can float through a cobweb of maggoty lines like a politician through pre-election promises. We sheared that lot like a scythe but I was far too busy ploughing into that dark and narrow crack between mole and cliff to more than note all the stomping about and frothing ashore. It was too shallow off that entrance for good health and a rapid build-up of seas was becoming far more alarming than the furore on the mole, for suddenly there was *Ben* up above me, balanced on the crest of a real thumper. He winked once, the fool, gripped the painter firmly between his teeth and surfed full pelt into *Lugworm*'s backside! I can tell you it was froth and pandemonium for a while, with nobody ashore trying to help one little bit.

But, of course, once within the lee there was nothing left bar the lolloping about with the sails flapping, so to ease the general tension I rowed mightily, following the line of that astonishingly long mole round a bend in the cliff which revealed a marvellously calm little basin, backed by yet another! It was just too good to be true, and I sang a little song as we gently took the bottom and started removing all the fish-hooks, floats and trailing lines from *Lugworm*'s underparts. Nobody came to see us, so I dripped about in the rain and finally accosted a lonely traffic warden. 'Where do I find the Harbourmaster?' I enquired. He looked me up and down, blew his nose, and replied in fervent Cornish, 'There ain't been no 'Arbourmaster here since Lord knows when ... back-along they was rummagin' for tin, shouldn't doubt!'

... under the ruin of Wheal Coates mine, Chapel Porth

'Well,' I explained, 'I've just come into the harbour. Shouldn't I notify somebody, maybe . . .?'

'Tell 'e what,' came the answer, 'go see old Jim down along the whelk stall, end of the car park there: e'll put 'e right.' And with a friendly pat he drifted off to book somebody.

Jim was stacking deckchairs disconsolately, the rain dripping off the ends of his moustache as I told him of my arrival.

'You'm in the 'arbour?' he asked with raised eyebrows.

'Yes.'

'Then you'm all right, then.' And he turned back to the chairs. Which seemed entirely satisfactory.

To be truthful I'm not really in love with that next bit of coast, some twenty-five miles down to Land's End. Nothing wrong with the coast – magnificent to look at – but from a dinghy it always gives me the impression of being . . . well, disinterested. Nothing to suggest it might help much if things went wrong. Those ghastly Stones a mile seaward of Godrevy heaving and baring their teeth and then the swollen knuckle of Cornwall's finger at Pendeen, where all the waters in the Bristol Channel sluice on the ebb round and out to the Western Approaches, as though Neptune had pulled the chain ... it's enough to give you the willies, and a fine old turmoil it can knock up just north of the Brisons with nothing but the fangs of the Longships to chew any bits of you that may be drifting to oblivion.

Then there's Sennen Cove. I know all about Sennen, having spent a week drawn up with the crabpots while the harbour turned into a maelstrom : it's no place to be in a northerly or nor'easter ... and bad enough in a nor'wester when there's any swell running. But you can't make the Scillies, twenty odd miles beyond the end of the Land on one ebb from Portreath. So Sennen it was next day on the morning ebb with a congenial pint in The Old Success while the cistern filled up again with the flood, and it was late afternoon on the top of the tide that we were nodding with the Longships and waiting for the ebb to help us out to an empty horizon. A sweet nor'easter came ruffling down from Wales and the sun even smiled once or twice : it couldn't have been fairer if we'd rigged the heavenly computer.

For those who sail westward, Reality proffers her visiting card at the Longships. The finale of that play, already rolling to its climax, finally dissolves in a crescendo of spume and froth on those last offlying reefs. Jagged and drowning under the onslaught, the iron jaw of the land flinches and gives slow ground before a relentless and ever encroaching sea.

The lighthouse rises, a monument to the changing of the scene. Behind, lies the hysterical half-real world of Man, totally wrapped in the Play, set at odds with the universe by his ego and diverted by his own shrewd activity. Ahead lies . . . ?

So the magic begins there and the Overture is an orchestration of silence. For most surely as our ears throw off the clamour of shore, so gradually do they become aware of that stillness which is an absence of all artificial sounds ... all hysteria ... all pressures. Only then can we begin to listen. So

31

we ghosted away from the land hand-in-hand with the ebb, and set course toward the southern shores of the group, for that way we knew we would carry a favourable stream for longer, and sail in less troubled waters than up northward of the isles.

'Have faith,' I said to *Lugworm*, for I sensed her apprehension as we headed for the empty horizon. 'Have faith, as I have faith in you . . . for we both know they are there, the islands, and we have but to trust our compass and the sea and the wind, and believe me, we shall arrive!'

So the sunlit hours passed. Astern, the world of man grew remote, and the lighthouse stood lonelier still, seeming to reach out as though yearning to voyage with us across that vast ocean whose edge it is condemned to watch – for ever. A single herring gull wheeled and circled, swooped and rose above *Ben* who was leaping and dancing astern, agog at the wonder of such a mighty sea, for the most he had known until then was the confines of the estuary and those frothing edges of the land . . . so slowly the evening light grew mellow, and the sea grew dark and still, and quietly gave us its promise to behave.

'Buggerlugs,' I whispered, for in moments of bliss such is the affectionate name to which she responds. 'Now there is nought but your thin skin 'twixt us and a merging back with that ocean from whence we both came . . . and to which we shall both, soon or late, most certainly return.' She chuckled quietly, for her soul understands these things, and above us the vast dome of the universe crackled into a thousand tiny points of starry laughter. It rippled down through the darkening eastern sky . . . and even *Ben*, doggedly biting on the painter in determination not to be left behind, seemed to wear a roguish grin as though he, too, were enjoying the thought.

So it was, there crept into us that gradual expansion of awareness which is beyond expression. Have you known this? Because I am a sailor I suspect such may only be experienced by mortal man when he is alone, under sail, in a very small boat on a very large ocean, and perhaps only in the timelessness of evening after the immediacy of day. Then – and even then only sometimes – may we drift upon reality all unsuspecting and glimpse her true expression . . .

The western sky took fire with a luminous green and the mirror edge of the sea over there burned the eyes. We voyaged in a dimension which is a hurt to mortal senses, and shadoward the sea grew dark, and *Lugworm*'s tan sails danced with their own ghosts in the moving water.

Three hours passed ... what strange yardsticks we do use ... three limitations of eternity took form, and northward against the luminous farewell rim of sky we saw the black silhouette of the Seven Stones lightship, and heard the sighing of the sea over that sunken continent of Lyonesse, and we floated in a world of half light, balanced delicately in a tension of in-between which spans polarity and gives rise to consciousness.

Lugworm was poised just midway between the light and the dark and stayed steady on that course careful not to strain too much for the one nor the other, for as I have said, her soul understands these things and she knew that, at this time, to seek either in its entirety meant losing awareness of them both ... and at another point in eternity we became aware of something other than sea and sky ahead. It was the daymark on St Martin's isle.

At first we both thought it to be the bridge of some supertanker, hull down, so bright did the tower gleam in the fading light. But it stayed on a steady bearing and grew clearer and nearer with the passing moments, and soon we could make out the sloping green top and bluff northern cliffs, and behind them the jagged outcrops of White Island, and shortly, beyond that, the boulder-hump of Round Island with the lighthouse sending its welcoming red beam every few seconds to greet us.

So calm was the sea, we altered a point northward straight for the Daymark, and gradually the islands grew in form and size, yet faded in detail, for the night was nearly upon us. Slowly the Hanjague – stark eastern sentinel – drew closer, breathed gently with the lapping of the sea around its base, and slid quietly past to our south. The warm scent of the isles came powerfully to us as we crept north of Nornour, and the black silhouettes of Chimney Rocks stared, but passed no comment on our presence.

The wind finally bid us adieu under the rise of Brandy

Point and the sails were already asleep as we rounded up under oars so as not to flout the silence. So it was that the gentle crunch of *Lugworm*'s keel on the sands of St Martin's came as both a sigh of content and an audible expression of thanks to the sea, and the wind, and the darkening sky, for a safe and perfect crossing.

Chapter Two

The Scillies

Cast a glance at the chart (page 36). You will see that the isles span a maximum distance of nine miles across their longest axis, roughly south-west/north-east from Bishop's Rock lighthouse to the Hanjague. Depths decrease quickly from some seventy metres a mile or so offshore to a mere metre in the shallow channel which sweeps round north of St Mary's isle. At low water equinoctial springs, between St Martin's and Tresco in that area south of Teän, there is no water at all other than isolated pockets, and the same applies in the wider southern part of the channel between Tresco and Bryher.

When making the isles from the eastward, the main and obvious approach to Hugh Town, capital of St Mary's isle, is through St Mary's Sound which is buoyed and carries a minimum depth of ten metres in the channel. You sweep round south of St Mary's, thence northward and eastward into the harbour, which is well protected from winds in the southerly and easterly quarters, but no place to be in a northerly or westerly gale, for in the latter case, added to the obvious sea and wind hazards there can come a rolling great swell which makes life aboard quite unromantic.

Scillonian, the ferryboat which plies between Penzance and the group, makes her low-water approach by this means, but at high tide she and other craft often choose to enter through Crow Sound to the north of St Mary's. By far the best anchorage for deep-keel yachts, in my opinion, lies off New Grimsby Harbour on the western side of Tresco. Here there are minimum depths of 2.4 metres nearly as far south as the quay wall, and excellent protection from the prevailing winds and swell with a permanent exit channel at all states of the

35

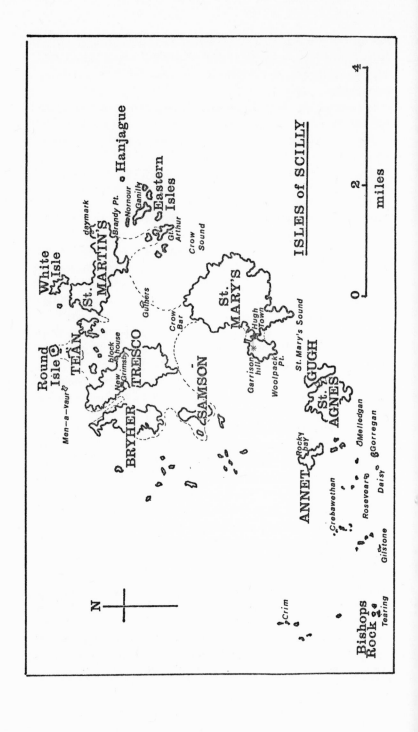

N

Round
Isle

White
Isle

Men—a—vaur

TEAN

BRYHER

New Grimsby
block house

TRESCO

St. MARTIN'S

daymark

Brandy Pt.

Nornour
Ganilly
Eastern
Isles

Hanjague

Gt.
Arthur

Crow
Sound

Guthers

SAMSON

Crow
Bar

St. MARY'S

Hugh
Town

Garrison
hill

Woolpack
Pt.

St. Mary's Sound

GUGH

St.
AGNES

Melledgan

Gorregan

Rocky
bay

Daisy

ANNET

Crebawethan

Rosevear

Gilstone

Crim

Bishops
Rock

Tearing

ISLES of SCILLY

0   2   4

miles

tide up northward when the weather serves. Admiralty metric chart number 34, scale 1 : 25,000 covers the whole group, and anyone attempting to navigate in this area without it is asking for trouble.

The range of the tide generally is around 5 metres (16.5 feet) at the top of springs and 2.3 metres (7.6 feet) at neaps, and the stream around the group is complex, directions swinging clockwise. High water at the isles may be taken at a rough average of five hours after high water Dover. At local high water the stream runs east-north-east then swings southerly, running roughly due south two hours after local high. Six hours after high (at local low water) it has swung generally in a westerly direction, swinging gradually up through north by three hours before the succeeding high water time, thereafter swinging gradually to an easterly set by the following high water. Such is the general flow around the group, but of course in between the isles a vast variety of directions is experienced depending on the configurations of the land.

Rates tend to be stronger north of the group, reaching four knots at springs just north of Tresco as opposed to around one and a half knots south of St Mary's, but in the narrows and over the shallows between the isles it can reach considerably more, and there are some fiendish races and overfalls up there off the northern shore.

For *Lugworm*, of course, with her minimum draught (plate and rudder up) of ten inches, virtually all areas of water are accessible provided there is no swell running, and she draws only eighteen inches with the outboard lowered. She is therefore the ideal craft in which to explore the isles, and there are few coves and grottoes that have not harboured her in the two extended summers I have spent there, camping aboard the boat.

That first morning after arrival, awakening with the rising sun, there came to me again a wonderful sense of wellbeing . . . of completeness, which islands always bring.

Lying in my sleeping bag on the cockpit bottomboards of *Lugworm*, I watched a rippling flow of reflected sunlight playing on the tent above. She was afloat – I could tell that, not from any lapping of water against the hull, but from the fact that she was on a level keel and the bright shimmering side of her tent would alternate first on port, then on starboard, as she swung slowly in an arc at the end of the anchor warp. Apart from this, we were in a motionless and soundless world, for there was no breath of wind, nor even the cry of a gull, so still was the dawn.

I lay there, watching the play of light for the best part of half an hour – which is the best way of waking up I know and guaranteed for putting you in fine affinity with Mother Nature and the whole world. After a while I raised myself on one elbow and peered aft through the open tent flaps. Two miles away, across a steel-bright mirror sea, the hump of Menawethan was silhouetted against the eastern horizon. Close northward and nearer, its southern flank part hiding Menawethan, was Great Ganilly, largest of the Eastern Isles. I watched awhile, willing *Lugworm* to swing her stern more southerly, and it seemed she must have sensed my wishes for very steadily my window on the world swung, scanning first a blaze of brilliance right beneath the sun and then taking in the humps of Little Ganilly, Great Arthur, Great and Little Ganinick, about half a mile away. There she stopped, the tent interior still irradiated with the direct rays and then gradually the stern swung slowly eastwards back towards Nornour.

'A north wind coming, if anything,' I told her, for she needs to know these things. 'That means we will have another day such as yesterday – and it'll be too good for wasting in the metropolis.' (A name we use when referring to Hugh Town, capital village of the isles).

Now I must tell you that over on the northern end of Great Arthur, there is a perfect little crescent-moon bay, fringed with a laugh of sand and flanked by granite boulders capped with Hottentot figs and marram grass. In fact it forms one side of a very narrow peninsula which joins Great Arthur to Little Arthur so that the two of them are really one island, though one should never tell them so. Only at very high springs does the peninsula become a shallow ford, with the stream swirling across and proclaiming aloud the lie to anyone who doubts their separate entities.

We know it as Hottentot Bay, on account of it being thick

with *carpobrutus edulis*, or Hottentot fig, and the best place to go when it's really hot, for you can run around naked as an aborigine if you choose, so thick is it with the absence of other souls.

'It's Hottentot today,' I proclaimed. 'We've potatoes aboard, fresh water, teabags, and if we can't hook a pollack 'twixt here and there we'll know we're growing rusty in the art.' So I started sorting out the trolling lines.

By the time it was all shipshape, the tent rolled forward about six feet to expose the afterdeck and a bit of the cockpit, a billy of tea brewed and drunk, why, that sun was giddy with height and laughing down on the world with a promise of glory. Ashore the island was waking up. A tractor engine puttered into life and there were echoes of distant voices far away over the hill.

So we motored, pollackless, over to Little Arthur. The tide was just past high springs and beginning to fall fast. I eased *Lugworm* gently on the rim of the beach and hooked her anchor securely behind a boulder to hold her safe while the tide drained out, then stripped to the sun and set off on the first voyage of exploration of the season. Not, mark you, that there is a great deal to explore, for the full length of Great and Little Arthur together is little more than three cables and half that in width. But they had everything I needed that day; most of all solitude and peace.

I ran across the peninsula, over a heather-swarded saddle where a Bronze Age grave gapes emptily up to the sky, and on up the grassy slopes of its eighty-foot pinnacle, highest point in the isle. The air was like sea-wine, so clear and fresh did it cut the lungs, and the dew on the shady side of the hill was still ice-cold on my bare feet and legs. But sunward the rocks and heather and grass were dry and warm, full of promise of long lazy hours to come. I tell you, it was a morning to remember.

Three blackbacks, startled from their sleepy perch on a rocky outcrop, launched vociferously off, swung in a wide circle and settled over on the barren sides of Ragged Isle away to the east. A colony of cormorants, alerted at the gulls' flight, stretched their necks enquiringly on the southernmost tip of Arthur Head and eyed me with suspicion. But the danger was not immediate: they kept a close surveillance on my movements, decided the time for flight had not yet arrived and settled once more to drying their outstretched wings, holding their arms out wide as they faced what cooling breeze there was to evaporate any moisture between their feathers.

From the top of the islet I could see the whole panorama of the isles laid out. There was a white yacht anchored off the old Blockhouse on Tresco two and a half miles away ... I could see the reflection of her hull shimmering in the sea over there, and the masts of local craft moored off Goats Point to the western end of St Martin's. Apart from that, the world seemed empty of folk, save me, which was just fine. I strolled back to Hottentot Bay, selected a soft grassy spot on the face of the dunes, inclined to the sun, took a blanket from the boat and settled down to enjoy the moment.

Have you ever listened to a small island waking up and adjusting to a hot summer day? It takes half an hour or so for the mind to empty itself. Round and round go the thoughts, darting out at a tangent, separating and taking 'you' off with them to environs quite out of harmony with the moment. But slowly it all subsides. You lie in the marram grass, breathing in the deep salty tang of its roots, with your eyes closed, and the warm sun glows gently hotter and hotter ... a faint wind swirls down through the spiky fronds, caressing your skin all over ... and silence takes the place of thought.

Silence.

So you gradually begin to hear it all. The whisper of grass above, where the marram fronds rustle in the air movement. A crackling nearby that's the very sound of growing things, stretching roots, splitting sheaths, and everywhere the faint awakening drone of insect life. At first it seems more like an overall murmur, unidentifiable until a singular quality of sound intrudes ... a scratching, urgent, methodical, as a black beetle unburies itself from the landslide of dry sand you disturbed while fossicking about with the blanket. Out come the front legs, waving in strange fashion as though belonging to a mechanical toy. A delicate feeler emerges, followed by another and then a head. For a moment it holds still, save for the trembling of the two feelers, as though taking stock of this upper world again after the sudden shock of burial. Then

40

the action begins in earnest, slow flailing legs work awkwardly at the sand, pushing the hard shiny body up, up, until at last completely emerged, it stands, sensing what's afoot. Now off it sets up a spike of grass – a hundred-and-fifty-foot tree, bending under its weight, falling scrabbling, on its back ... a determined steady heaving of the heavy body as it prises at the shifting sand to right itself ... and again the mechanical onslaught up the grass. What will it do, I wonder, when it reaches the tip? But it never does: it deflects along another spike and slowly makes off through the boles of the forest ... after what? Why do I ask? Perhaps unknowing, it's completely content simply just being a beetle.

Somewhere down on the wet shingle of the peninsula, where the receding tide has forsaken it, a crab is scuttling. You hear its tiny 'plopping' like bursting bubbles – I'm sure crabs belch! – and the exposed weed, drying in the ever-increasing heat, keeps crackling and popping. The sound of a myriad winged insects forms a background to the play, and far distant there is the occasional strident call of a gull. A bee buzzes urgently past ... there is the sudden startled flurry of wings as an oystercatcher, about to alight on the beach, sees this alien form and sheers off in surprise. But you lie perfectly still, merging into the isle itself, and gradually the wild things become accustomed to your intrusion.

A couple of gulls wing across, in desultory conversation. There is a steady zephyr wind now, flowing over the dune above you, swaying the grass in a moving green pattern against the pure blue of the sky, and the sand is warming up, absorbing and radiating back the heat. You turn over, exposing your back to the sun, burying your nose into the roots of the grass over the edge of the blanket, and breathe the pungent air deeply. Things get hazy in a warm cocoon of content ...

Waking up is a surprise. Have you really been asleep at all? Or were you just partly switched off? There's a parched dry feeling on the back of your neck, down your back and in the soft part of the backs of your knees. You wriggle gently, stiff and aching from lying so long in one position, and slowly your limbs flow back to life. Up on one elbow, and the world is a blinding hurt, too bright to open the eyes fully. Everything looks flat and white in the brilliance. You feel like a lump of wood, stiff and hard-jointed. Slowly you grow more flexible as you sit up, on an alarmingly sore bottom, and there is Alphonse staring at you from a circular predatory gull's eye, turning his head first to get a view from the left, then the right.

He is the only large moving thing in the scene, apart from yourself. You continue to eye one another, in mutual curiosity.

'Morning, Alphonse.' He turns his head quickly sideways and brings the other eye into use, a degree of suspicion hovers about his pristine white and grey form.

'What's it like being a herring gull?'

He pecks himself quickly under one wing, then brings the other eye to bear: 'What's it like to be hungry . . . that's what it's like to be a gull!'

'Are you always hungry?'

'Always.'

'Life's one long search for food then?'

'Nothing but.'

'Boring?'

'Certainly not. It's never boring searching for food. Appetite is everything. Without appetite life would be pointless. With appetite you've got a purpose for living; assuagement of appetite. It's very satisfying . . . very pleasant . . . are you, then, so very different?'

I think about that. Somewhere far off in another world comes the drone of the morning helicopter from the landing pad on St Mary's. The tide has withdrawn, leaving the isles robed with a skirt of damp seaweed. It lies like drowned hair in long fronds over the top of the still water.

But Alphonse seems to be waiting for an answer.

'I've got intelligence,' I tell him.

'I've got instinct,' he counters. 'Instinct for survival – that's worth a bucketful of intelligence.'

'You miss the point,' I tell him. 'Intelligence can be more useful than instinct alone. Look at me, I'm a human. My brain is many times greater than yours. I can THINK. I have modified my environs not only to survive, but also to suit myself. I have tilled the land, tamed the face of earth, built up a technology that takes the slavery from mere existence. I'm capable of depths of sorrow, heights of bliss. Life for me is

42

more than simple survival. It has subtlety, poignancy, exquisite delicacy of feelings. It's a rich tapestry of experiences. It's brought greater freedom of action—'

'Freedom to destroy yourselves,' Alphonse interrupted. 'You haven't learned when to stop.'

'To stop what?'

'To stop raping the earth, to control your own propagation and appetites. You think you're free, but you're in greater slavery than I. I have no problems like that, I leave it to nature, she takes care of it. With your so-called intelligence you've interfered with the order of things and you're exploiting your environs on a short-term spree. Using up earth fast. Is that intelligent?'

I thought about that.

'I'm not sure I like you much,' Alphonse continued. 'Things were fine before your species came along, and now look at it . . . things are different in a sick sort of way, and getting sicker. As a species, you humans are a cancer in a limb of the universe. Grasping, overrunning, transforming everything to the exclusive advantage of homo sapiens in fine disregard for the balance of the total organism. Like a cancer you're thriving at a suicidal rate. Like a cancer you'll eventually kill the organism. I give you thirty years at the most, and you'll be the end of us all. Intelligent . . . huh!'

I thought about that too, and suddenly I was annoyed. I didn't want to look truth in the face this morning – I'd come to the isles to escape all that for a week or two and here was this blasted gull reminding me of it. I sat up and hissed. Alphonse squirted off.

It hurt, sitting up quickly like that. I'd overdone it a bit and roasted myself behind, but I can take any amount of sun, really, never peel much or go rotten, just brown. My father had malaria, blackwater, yellow water and every damned fever you care to name back on the Gold Coast and passed on to me some pigmentation in the skin that's burn-proof and gnat-proof. Mosquitoes loathe the smell of me: it's splendid.

Lugworm was high on the rim of the dried-out beach and roasting hot under the tent. I rolled back a foot or two of the canvas at the bow to allow a free circulation of air. Even *Ben*, upside down on a bank of Hottentot figs, seemed to be

43

gasping: the day was turning into a scorcher. I stood on my head for a moment, just for fun and to get the blood re-circulating, lavered myself with sun-oil and took stock. Eleven a.m. and getting hotter: only one thing for it – fresh fish for supper! We had been unsuccessful on the trip across, so what better than a quiet, predatory hunt to pass away the stuporific hours . . . and wasn't *Ben* gasping for coolth? I hooked a fat juicy winkle, sorted out a line, carried *Ben* down to the bottom of the bay and pushed him quietly off, careful to soften any sharp sound of oar on rowlock. Outside the entrance of the bay the weed strung out in twenty-foot streamers, like green mermaid's hair trailing on the surface. The bottom, five feet down, was a limpid world of wonder: tall trees waved softly above fields of water ferns, deep pools of shadow harboured ghost shapes that dissolved by the mere act of inspection.

Have you ever lain timeless in a coracle-skiff with your nose half an inch above the mirror surface, drifting silently with the stream, your eyes probing down into the quivering green cool littoral below? You haven't? A pity. It's magic. Like floating in a silent balloon, peering down on a fantasy land-scape, you drift effortlessly above the filmy transluscent tops of green forests. Shafts of light, toned from surface brilliance to muted blue-green depth, sink down into fields of levitating forms, spreading their many coloured shapes to catch the life-giving light. Gossamer-thin curtains of opaque green hang undulating slowly in the stream. Devoid of brute gravity, forms akin to those ashore float in serene weightlessness. Here there is, in microcosm, the towering conifer, but its trunk is glowing gold and the tips of its needle branches radiate pale-blue light. Cliffs of pink and cream rock drop from im-measurable heights to bottomless pits of dark nothingness, their crevasses holding the tenacious fronds of some strange aquatic gorse, and here, from a dense undergrowth of gently waving tendrils, come the boles of pampas grass. But their cylindrical trunks do not branch or taper, but rise like thick snakes up . . . up . . . up from the depths to within an inch of your nose, and then, at the extremity of their supporting world, turn and bask, yard after yard of them, on the sea's face.

You hold your breath, so as not to stir the window surface

44

and destroy the clarity of this magic world, and gently, as you drift away from the shore, the forests recede. Deeper, darker, the colours fade and the forms become strangely more primaeval... thick rubbery arms clutch up at you from dark gorges, their extremities spreading into grotesquely frill-fingered hands of mauve-brown kelp. Macabre contorted roots, spotted, twisted and fungoidal peep through the leathery foliage... and ... AH!

A movement. Quick, dartlike, you see movement down there beneath those slimy leaves. Carefully you ease an arm over the side of *Ben*, squeeze a trailing line of the green mermaid's hair, and wait. The hairs gently incline, tauten, and you are anchored, moving now silently through the water but motionless over the bottom. Yet even that slight, scarcely detectable tautening of the trailing weed has transmitted an alarm. A swirl of water in motion betrays the flight: yet you see no fin, nor shiny scale, simply the quick kick sideways of one small frond of weed down there near the roots. That is all. So somewhere nearby, the cause of it is still there, waiting, hiding in the water forest, and you watch...

Ben's shadow shafts down on the kelp. It has an etheric aura of blue lining its rim, a halo of light caused by some freak of refraction, as his movement against the stream forms a tiny ripple. This, too, must be signalling an alarm. But so long as it stays constant, without change, the alarm systems will cease. You lie still as the floating weed... and watch. The sun is burning hot on your back but the oil is doing its work, soothing the slight soreness. Somewhere up and far away, beyond the rim of your present world, an urgent beat startles the silence. The sharp rapid slap of wings on water. A cormorant eases its ungainly form into the air. You don't move; this is a natural sound that will not trigger off any alarms... but one thoughtless twitch on your part and the quarry will be gone. Minutes pass. Your sight wanders slowly through the weed, looking without looking, as though the mere fact of concentration will somehow transfer itself to alert the sensitive form below.

Then you see it!

A shape, dark and smoky brown, the exact colour of the kelp. Isn't that a head? You scan the form of it, motionless down there, and there is something too regular in the matching of those slight bulges, one at either side. Are they not eyes? A faint, scarcely discernible rhythmic expansion and contraction – the gills quietly working. A pollack? The long body is hidden back in the kelp roots ... what size is it? Difficult to guess, size is misleading under water, but well worth catching.

A tingle of excitement runs through every fibre of you as quietly, slowly, without any jerks, you lower the winkle-baited hook. It streams infuriatingly away with the tide, then gently filters down toward the kelp. There's a tiny lead weight about two feet from the hook. You let it reach the bottom, keeping your eyes on the winkle, then gently ease it up a little, jigging it very, very gently up and down. The winkle lifts and falls, dancing down-tide from the weight. Pollack is aware of all this, but lying doggo, still as the weed roots.

You jiggle on. About six feet up-tide he's watching, curious. Can he smell it? Can fish smell? How well can they see? Will he see the line? You keep your arm inside the boat, so as to throw no moving shadow down there. Your neck is stiff with the effort of watching, motionless. Nothing happens. You jiggle on. He's watching, too.

Watching!

Your left hand is cramped with holding the weed, your arm aches with the rigidity but you dare not make a single twitch. Sound travels through water too well: he'd be off. This is the critical moment ... he's being lulled. Nothing is happening and that means safety. You watch those gills, hypnotic in their gentle expansion and contraction. Are those eyes looking at you? How does a fish see? He's alert, that's for sure: something in the way he's holding himself tells you that. Is he aware of that winkle? Strange: he's growing in size as you watch. Jumping Jeesups it's a whacker! He hasn't moved, and yet now you can see the whole dark, almost transparent lithe line of his body; he's drifting out of the weed. Drifting? Against the stream? Now you can see how it happens ... a faint, slow swing of the tailfin and that electrifying form glides without appearing to glide, then, still as a drifting log begins to sweep down with the tide toward winkle. Not a movement, not a suggestion of motion anywhere ...

46

just a dark line of intensely alert, curious fish. There's obviously something odd about that winkle. I send a telepathic command singing down the line ... 'Come and eat me ... come on, I'm the best dinner you've set eyes on for ...' Quick ... quicker than the eye can see he's flashed across stream, and the line's singing away. I gasp, grab the line and heave. There's an electrifying, galvanising jerk ...

... and slackness!

Sod it. I pull in the empty hook. Sodsbleeding bodkins, after all that, and he got away with a free dinner. Must have been ten pounds if an ounce. Maybe twenty. How big do pollack grow? Was it a pollack after all ... was it, perhaps, a dogfish? Or a small shark? Enormous! Quivering with tension and frustration I grab the oars and row violently back, glad to feel muscles moving again. As I close the bay, a flock of herring gulls lifts from *Lugworm*'s afterdeck ... Heathen Furies, they've been at my bread. I left a loaf on the sidedeck and it's reduced to a battered heap of crumbs. Dammit, and I bet that was Alphonse at the head of them. One up to Alphonse!

We learn. We learn to cover a catch of mackerel with a bucket if we leave the boat untended, or they'll be gone, and serve us right, for it's all part of the game of survival. We have intelligence, we ought to know these things.

But it's not so bad. There's another loaf in the locker and a bottle of yellow plonk with a simply magnificent label to wash down the cheese and sardines, and all afternoon to sleep it off in the sun – on my back.

So early evening drifted in. With it came the rising tide, and *Lugworm* soon swung at the end of her warp again. We motored across to Higher Town to arrange for fresh milk, place a request for a loaf of bread (if one extra could be made at the next bake) and retreated back to Great Arthur.

On the way we land a fine mackerel!

Only the stars are competing now with the red glow of my driftwood fire. Its flames throw a dancing light on the boulders close about, and *Ben* is propped to windward, a shield from the cool night air. *Lugworm*'s tent is a faintly lighter patch out there in the bay, swinging gently on the end of her anchor warp, and my Aburöken smoker is turning that mackerel into the most exquisite tasty morsel a vagabond could pray for! The billy of potatoes is nearly ready and the pungent scent of the oaken sawdust under the mackerel vies with that pure fresh wholesome smell of the burning logs. A silence has fallen on the dark world. Its borders have blended into the infinity of night . . . and I'm alone in a cocoon of orange flickering light, with all summer ahead.

A good first day in the isles?

Oh yes, it could have been worse!

'What, or who, precisely, determines whether a pile of guana-covered rocks shall be just rocks, or island?' I asked the bearded piratical character in the Mermaid Inn about a week after arriving in Hugh Town. Through the window I could see a three-masted French barquentine anchored out in the roads. Square-rigged on the foremast, and fore-and-aft rigged on the main and mizzen, she was flying the Red Ensign courtesy fashion from the starboard yardarm and had baggy-wrinkles galore on the topping lifts. It lifted the heart to see her, the beauty. A score or so of smaller French and English plastic yachts of all shapes and sizes were dotted about, making a fine colourful showing, and I could see the Harbourmaster clearing a berth for *Scillonian*, due in within half an hour.

The pirate looked at me hard, took a swig from the pint pot, wiped his beard, and said nothing. But I wasn't to be fobbed off with strategy.

'It says here,' and I prodded a leaflet on the Scillies in my most belligerent manner, 'that there is an isle for every day of the year. That makes three hundred and sixty-five islands. It seems about three hundred too many by my reckoning. Who exactly determines what's an island and what's a rock?'

He slammed the pint pot down with a bang. 'Me and you,' he hissed.

'Then so far as I'm concerned,' I countered, 'Guthers out there is a rock, not an island.'

'That's right, Guthers is an island.' So we drank to the wisdom of it and I wandered off down the quay where *Lugworm* was being jostled by a pert plastic pimp of a boat with pale pink sails. She looked uncomfortable. A brisk northerly was making things merry in the harbour, burgees were a-chatter and crews alert. Up to windward Tresco looked green and washed, the long white sweep of her southern strand like a Cheshire-cat grin snug in the lee of the isle. A group of youngsters were fishing from the very tip of the quay on Rat Isle and we hoped together unproductively for a few moments, until the distant hoot of *Scillonian* wafted me out of now into a far away then. I have a soft spot for *Scillonian*, and for a very good reason. It was aboard her, twelve years ago, that I first set eyes on B. We had both come to the isles for the first time, by way of a desperate attempt to escape from a problematical way of life in which we were getting enmeshed. It was early March, 1962, and bitter cold. *Scillonian* was berthed at Penzance and I was roaming the south coast rather aimlessly. Seeing her there I decided to come across for a couple of days just to get even farther away from everything. I remember thinking the ship looked a bit dreary and forlorn against the cold grey stones of Penzance quay that morning and the gangway, making an alarming angle down on to her afterdeck, was groaning morbidly.

A figure in a ghastly puce coat was feeding two dirty swans with stale railway sandwiches from a paper bag. I lumbered down the gangway, walked around the deck a few times, only to find the ship apparently deserted except for that solitary form. I sidled up.

'They look a bit dejected,' I said, to raise the tone of communication.

She didn't even look at me. 'Not hungry,' said a soft female voice. And that was that. End of conversation. I wandered off to look for the saloon, but it was locked until sailing time in an hour or so, and altogether things were a bit dismal. Out of a steely grey sky, a penetrating north-easter was sweeping through the town and across the harbour, investing the sea with that icy indifference to all living things that such conditions can. I was cold, and getting colder. The puce coat was still leaning over the taffrail aft, looking at the swans. But I felt my presence didn't bring any joy there: something in the tone of voice, the unconcealed indifference, warned me to keep my distance. I set to walking briskly round the decks, down the long, covered, dark colonnade between the ship and the

dripping quay wall, across the foredeck, up the brighter colonnade on the side away from the quay, and across her afterdeck. Round and round. Round and round. I started counting
the steps, up one side, down the other. Then, to break the
monotony, started counting the steps walking backwards. It's
astonishing what a difference the length of a backward step
can be.

A discreet cough.

There, at the far end of the weather colonnade was an embarrassed puce coat, walking towards me. I know exactly
what was going through her mind. 'Must be well over thirty,
if a day. Seemed quite normal, what a tragedy. Wonder
what eventually tipped the balance. Just act as if everything is
O.K. There'll be a few more people aboard in a moment and
it'll be quite all right . . .'

I turned, and started walking in a forward direction down
the long colonnade towards her. Have you ever actually walked
slowly down a long colonnade toward a solitary person who is
walking slowly toward you down the same colonnade? At
first you pretend to be oblivious of each other. You look over
the side, up in the air, at your watch, scratch behind your
ears, tie your shoelace, and they do exactly the same, in different order. The inevitable thing is that when finally you
glance at them to see whether they're looking at you, they're
always glancing at you to see if you're looking at them!

It's something to do with our social upbringing, and vanity.
You see it when two strangers meet at a party without
introduction – always slightly embarrassed because neither
knows the correct conventional groove to slot into – the correct rules to be observed with the total 'stranger'. But I had
the advantage here : I knew she was convinced I was mad. I
played on it, unfairly perhaps. I locked my eyes on to hers,
and simply kept looking into them as we approached each
other. At first she followed the conventional pattern of avert-
ing her own gaze instantly, whenever it met mine, but as my
unconventional manner was imprinted on her attention things
began to change. Her eyes stayed looking into mine. She
stopped walking. They narrowed a little, peering . . . I continued walking slowly toward her. An aura of real alarm now
emanated from her, masked instantly by a conscious effort to

50

appear natural again. But of course it was no good. The poor girl began to dissolve into open panic.

'It's quite all right,' I laughed. 'No need to be alarmed, I'm almost normal really . . . just bored stiff, and wishing the bar was open. It looks as if we're to be the only two passengers to the isles today!'

The relief was good to see. Obviously, though perhaps not exactly 'normal', I was, possibly, not exactly 'dangerous' either. At that moment the clank of feet on metal steps lumbered up from somewhere in the nether regions of the ship. A key turned in the public saloon door down the corridor and a face peered out. 'Aha!' I bellowed. She jumped. 'Coffee?' said the face. I swept her into the saloon.

After that things were better. *Scillonian* eventually bumbled out from the quay, set her bows seaward, and the land began to recede astern. It was biting cold. So far as I can remember we were the sole passengers, but my perception may have been narrowed somewhat by events. We settled down in the lee of the port side on one of those peculiar seafaring seats of slatted bars that have strange galvanized tanks built beneath them. I've often wondered what the psychological effect would be after a traumatic maritime disaster to float about the oceans of the world on a buoyant park seat.

I looked at her. She was a bit thin, worn and pale. She had a sort of fishing-net cap in off-white wool pulled down over her ears and there were mouse-coloured curls with flecks of blonde in them pushing out here and there round the rim. The collar of that hideous victoria-plum coat hid her neck and she wore a pair of black woollen gloves and wellington boots over corduroy trousers. She looked desperately tired, and rather miserable, but there was something about her eyes that caught you . . . something transparently real, frightfully vulnerable, completely honest. Something that said, without speaking one word to me, 'Look, I know you're bored stiff, I know I'm the only bird on the boat and you wouldn't look at me twice if there were a selection. In a way I'm grateful for your attention because it's always pleasant for a woman to receive the attention of a man . . . but just now, I'm not in the running: I'm tired and fed-up and want a bit of solitude. Please don't pester me.'

51

I understood. There was, however, a point on which I would have disagreed with her had she said that in so many words. In any company, in any crowd, those eyes and my reactions would have been the same.

So we crouched on the slatted seat with our backs against the white-painted cabin side and looked across that endless grey sweep of Atlantic, and a sleety drizzle that was turning to snow began to sweep horizontally across the sea. The smoke from dear old *Scillonian*'s funnel drifted away from us, mingling with the sleet, and our world was enormous, drear and grey.

'Never mind,' I said, after a bit. 'I always remember that when things start badly, by simple law of chance, they'll almost certainly improve! Are you going to be on the island long?' I was almost afraid to ask, for the last thing I wished was to be a nuisance.

She didn't smile. 'A week . . . and you?'

'Couple of days at the most, I think. I've not booked in anywhere . . . counting on the guest houses being empty at this time of year. Are you fixed up?' Was this being a nuisance? She could always switch me off with a rebuff.

'Yes, I'm booked in at . . . hm! Forgotten the name of the place, but I've got the address somewhere. It's on St Mary's, but I've never been there before so it's all a bit of a pig in the dark . . . I mean a . . . a . . .'

'A pig in a poke,' I said. She laughed. Oh, this was better. I remember suddenly a rift in the grey pall moved across the sun's face, and a heartwarming shaft of light picked out the snowflakes against the grey sky and waves. It was unbelievably beautiful. Thousands upon thousands of flecks of glowing light drove over the face of the sea. I got up and looked to weather away from the sun. 'Gosh,' I called to her, 'look – quick!'

Two concentric half circles of diffuse colour – one of the most perfect double rainbows I've ever seen – arched from the dark face of the sea up against a thunder-black sky and down again. We stood together looking at it. 'Do you know,' I said, 'you're not seeing the same rainbow as I . . . everybody sees a different rainbow because their eyes are in a slightly different position in relation to the refracted light.'

There was a long silence. She was standing beside me, and

the two of us were huddled against the sleet, our faces into the wind.

I knew she was looking at me. For the first time, really looking at me, and all my life I shall remember what she said.

'I think that's a pity. I wish you hadn't told me that ... anyway, it's beautiful just the same.'

Scillonian rumbled on. The sun withdrew, the sea closed in all round us and we began to roll as she eased out from the lee of the Cornish peninsula, out into the long swell mountains that undulate through the channel between the isles and the Land's End.

Two hours later we were both glad when she got into the lee of the group. Dark and uninviting they looked, a ragged black line etched on the horizon up to weather, but they kept that mountainous swell at bay, and the old ship held herself more steady as we swept into the entrance to St Mary's Sound. The quay at Hugh Town was deserted except for a few lorries stacked with island produce, waiting to be loaded. *Scillonian* shunted back and forth, the lines snaked across and the gangway clattered down. She stood with a huge suitcase against the ship's rail. I had a small grip holding nothing more than towel, swimsuit and a couple of jerseys.

'No transport?' I queried.

'No. But I don't think I need it anyway. My lodgings are in Hugh Town somewhere, so it can't be far.'

She struggled down the gangway, and dropped the case at its foot. It had stopped snowing, and the cloud was breaking up but the wind was even stronger, keeping the gulls aloft, screaming in derision at we shivering mortals. She picked up the case again in the other hand.

This was the critical moment. I had to come right out in the open and put my cards on the table. 'Look,' I said. 'Believe me, the last thing I would wish is to force my attention on you or be a nuisance. But please let me carry that case into the village – to your lodgings, wherever they are. When we get there, if you'd rather, I'll buzz off and find somewhere for myself. If you really don't care either way, I'd like to book in where you are staying, if they have room.'

She looked at me, and I looked at her. 'Thanks for being so honest, and for the offer. I like both the ideas.'

It was a devil of a long way to the lodgings. Right through the town and up the hill and that case wasn't light. She carried mine, I carried hers, and guess which one of us was sweating before we arrived. There was room at the inn. The sun had come out in a light washed sky and the wind was blasting the islands dry. We walked that afternoon round Garrison Hill, the promontory just west of Hugh Town. It was exciting, following the old garrison walls, looking down the dry moat of Star Castle Hotel, the Elizabethan fortress built in the form of an eight-pointed star. Stretched on the grass at Woolpack Point, we listened to the haunting toll of the bell buoy on Spanish Ledges. The sea rolled white-capped and laughing out of the Sound, and we were strangers, and far away from everything and happy.

How do you get to know another person? Are you searching all the while? Not consciously, I think. Was I aware even then that her hands fascinated me? The long thin fingers, the slim delicacy of the palms and wrists? She was tall and slim this girl, with strong bold eyebrows in an intelligent face. A Londoner, on the editorial staff of a magazine...B.A. at Durham...all the qualificational paper trappings to efficiently wrap-up a splendid twentieth-century 'career'. A fine intact shell complete. But somehow, as she said afterwards, at that time the kernel seemed to be missing.

That first afternoon was the only sun we saw. The weather broke during the night, and breakfast next morning was dawdled over to the rattle of rain on the windows and the howl of a near gale. We took a packed lunch and set off in jeans and oilskins for Peninnis Head, extreme southern tip of St Mary's.

I remember sitting in the lee of a granite monolith looking across to St Agnes and Gugh. The screaming demented wind had swung to the south-east, driving a seething mass of grey spume up the sound. An awe-inspiring swell had built up, crashing in terrible fury on the Bow and Spanish Ledges. The southern flank of Gugh was drowned under solid sheets of water. Westward we could hear the power of it thundering over Carrickstarne rocks, and the headland itself seemed to shake to the onslaught. 'This is exceptional, even for Cornwall,' I told her. It was dry under the overhanging bluff, but the sky was a fury of shredded cloud and the wind was rising still. That was 7th March 1962, and I doubt the islanders will forget it. By noon a full hurricane was blasting the group *Scillonian*, trapped and with double warps rigged, heaved uneasily in the lee of the mole. The quay at Penzance was unusable due to the end of it being smashed and toppled into her berth. No helicopter could get airborne. Telephone communication was cut. We crawled on hands and knees against the fury of it over Peninnis Head, working our drenched way along the weather shore, scrambling and sliding down grassy slopes, cowering behind great bluffs of granite, rolling in sheer excitement and exultation at the power of the wind.

But alas the tide was rising. A sea such as was running that evening does little damage when it drives to death on the lower rockstrewn extremities of a shore, but at high water it's a different story. The swell, rolling in from open sea, builds up in height as it feels the shallowing bottom, rears as it approaches the land, and crashes in devastating power at the very highest point of the beaches. In its path lay Old Town, with a stout protective sea wall running round part of the little bay. By evening it was carnage. The wall itself had cracked, hammered by hundreds of tons of driving solid water, and then, undermined, it had broken up completely. The road through Old Town became a river of rushing water. Roofs were torn off. Sandbags were filled and all emergency crews brought into action. At Porthcressa Beach the seas washed clean across the peninsula, flooding the shops and houses in Hugh Town and sweeping small craft through into the grassy Park in front of the Town Hall.

There was, thank heaven, no loss of life, and the islanders swung to with a will to clear up the mess, but still the wind kept up its wild dirge. On the third day of the storm we walked the entire coast of St Mary's, and I remember, when it came on to rain again, taking shelter in an eroded section of a low cliff near Bant's Carn looking across toward St Martin's. We tried to get a driftwood fire going, but the wood, grass, and air itself was soaked. The isles lay bleached with wind and water.

Often I wonder whether we would, but for that gale, have

found time to explore each other's minds as we did. Five days we were marooned on St Mary's, walking the isle, drenched and battered by those winds, and finally *Scillonian* got the 'all clear' from Penzance. On the sixth day we re-embarked.

I left her at Penzance railway station. 'No sentimental partings,' we agreed. 'Particularly not on railway stations.' So we said good-bye. 'Write if you get time.' 'Thanks for a wonderful five days.' 'See you again, of course – sometime in town.'

All that . . . and all that . . . So I went to collect my car. It was the end of a strange, oddly disturbing five days, and suddenly, as I drove through the town, I felt desperately, unbelievably, lonely. I stopped at a garage to top up the tank, and before I swung out of the forecourt the decision was made. Back through the town I drove hell-for-leather down to the docks area and pulled up adjacent to that wall that separates the higher road from the station down below. I jumped from the car, ran to the wall and peered down. A train was in . . . but was it hers?

Desperately I scanned the platform. It was deserted except for a couple of station staff. Obviously the train was within seconds of starting. Then I saw her. She was leaning on the open sill of a door looking down at the platform. I sprinted along the pavement until I was opposite, and called. As I did so, the guard blew his whistle. She didn't hear me. I called again. She looked up and saw me, and the train was moving off . . .

'B.' I yelled, running to keep abreast. 'Would you marry me if I asked you?'

The train gave a deafening blast of sound. She was still looking up at me as I ran along that wall top. I saw her lips moving but could hear nothing. But she was smiling. Had she understood?

I just stood there, watching that train trundle her away with an ear-shattering hoot . . . and here was old *Scillonian* nosing in from the Sound, shunting back and forth. The lines snaking out and the gangway rumbling down . . .

The telephone box below Castle Gate was draughty and far from soundproof. 'B.,' I said, '*Lugworm* needs you . . .'

56

A Thorn Apple found on Teän. Instant death if you eat it!

You don't stay in St Mary's Port with a northerly spanking in ... not in a small boat, anyway, for there are far better places to be. I kissed the phone good-bye, bought a pint of milk and rowed out in *Ben* to unship *Lugworm*'s tent and step the masts. Then we weighed and motored up to Teän, halfway between St Martin's and Tresco.

Of all the isles, Teän is my favourite, for it's inaccessible at low water in any normal craft, and I can let *Lugworm* dry out near the top of the tide and know she's safe, come hell, 'till next high water – and the isle is mine. Uninhabited, it's under half a mile in length, but affords a splendid lee no matter from what direction storms may come. Teän Sound, a narrow gully some four and a half metres in depth, divides the isle from Goats Point on the western extremity of St Martin's and it's not more than a cable and a half across, so in good weather I can easily make it under oars in *Ben*. The other way – westward across to Tresco – things are a bit more difficult. There's a jawful of jagged teeth ready to chew you to bits if you don't know the channels. The walls of a ruined cottage stand on the south shore of Teän, and I berthed up in the bay there, beneath them for the night.

Dawn found the northerly breathed away, and a still calm day forecast, so for fun *Ben* and I rowed round the isle's west shore, then struck north for Round Island, for I had a whimsey to see the Lighthouse and pass the time of day with the keepers. It's not more than a mile and a good flex of the muscles up through St Helen's Gap, past the sightless cadaver of the isolation hospital where the unfortunate crews of sailing craft in old times were put ashore with fever. Across the 'Pool' and round Didley's Point we skimmed, *Ben* with a bone in her teeth, eager to close the Camber Rocks south of Round Island. An interesting place this, for the steps from the lighthouse come tumbling down the steep southern slope of the isle to a small terrace in the cliff. From here a stout overhead wire has been rove to the peak of the offlying rocks and doubtless in rough weather the supply craft use this to cast a line over, for in such conditions it could be a dangerous business to close the rocky buttresses of the isle itself. The wire was high out of my reach, however, and the best I could do was secure *Ben*'s painter to a rung of the vertical ladder leading up to the terrace, making due allowance for the rising tide. My approach had been spotted. Down the steps, hell-for-leather, came a figure running. Aha, thinks I, I'm to be told it's private property and 'Be off with me!' But nothing such. A cheery wave and the cry, 'Any fags aboard,' was the worst broadside I got. Fags! – me in a swimsuit and *Ben* sloppy with inquisitive sea! No, alas, I had no fags nor have any use for them. But I found the lighthouse and her crew most interesting. The adjacent signal flagstaff particularly so, for I learned a trick from it. Winds have a habit of changing direction, you may have noticed. If you're flying flags, they tend after a bit to get fouled up with halyards and other gear aloft, but not here – the flag halyard was attached at its lower end not to the staff but to a massive iron cannonball. After hoisting the signal, you just dragged the ball away from the foot of the mast till the halyard and the flags flew clear and free. If the wind changed its mind, all you had to do was shift the cannonball round.

There was a bit of a swell running down from the north, residue of yesterday's blow, and Eastward Ledge just seaward of the isle was breaking into a creamy grin occasionally, but the sea was smooth as a baby's bottom and there was little sign of any trouble arising. Half a mile south-west of Round Island is a fearsome isolated crag of rock called Men-a-Vaur. Forty-odd feet above high water springs it towers like three great molars, and there's a dark chasm, sheer-sided and not more than ten feet broad that splits it near in half. Now I've sailed round Men-a-Vaur times enough, at a respectful distance, for the fringe of white water round her skirts keeps any prudent craft at bay. But today I'd caught her sleeping: true there was a healthy rise and fall of swell working away on her northern face, but to the south side, where that chasm split into her, it was quieter. This is a haunt of the cormorant and blackback, and I had a mind to take a close look at the whitened tops of those fangs. 'If we work in just yonder where that ledge will afford us a footing, and you jump up smartly on my back before the swell recedes,' I told *Ben*, 'dammit, we'll be high and dry before the next swell comes rolling in.' And so it worked out. I eased *Ben* over the ledge when there was about three feet of water on it, rolled out quick and swung him up on my shoulders before the crest withdrew, and there he was climbing like a two-legged beetle sedate as you could wish out of the reach of Old Father Neptune's next lick.

After I parked him, it was a stiff ascent, back-a-knee up some of the vertical rifts, and inclined to be greasy with the guana, and a bit smelly, but on the very peak, why I was king of the isles, with a thousand screaming gulls proclaiming me so, circling in a sonic crown up there above my head, and it was a wild, grand moment, and good to be alive. I dare not tarry long, for one small change in the mood of the sea and it would be too much for *Ben*. Launching the skiff was yet more fun for I made a wholesome mess of it. I placed his wooden skeg carefully on the limpet-encrusted ledge, careful to keep the delicate painted skin off the needlesharp points, and waited for the swell to float him before leaping in. Trouble with swell is, it doesn't just go up and down – it swirls in horizontally as well, and as *Ben* floated he was swept off that ledge before I could quite get all of me aboard. And *Ben* wasn't having just part of me aboard!

Up he tilted, in I went, and there were the two of us awash in that chasm with the sky above a ringing peal of bird laughter. But being made of planks *Ben* stays as buoyant as myself, and I towed him back to the ledge and set to work putting that water back where it belonged. While at this I spied a tragedy taking place at the foot of the rocks opposite side of the chasm. A young herring gull – couldn't have been hatched more than a few days – had somehow got things round the wrong way and become too familiar with Neptune before courting the zephyrs. Whatever the cause, the poor thing was in the water desperately trying to regain a footing on the rocks, completely waterlogged and obviously exhausted and near to drowning. There was a fine commotion going on overhead where the family were strident with advice, but the poor thing no sooner got a footing than the next wave swiped him off, and he was past making much real effort. I relaunched *Ben*, edged him across, waited for the right moment and grabbed the chick. Too far gone to stand, he lay quivering in a soggy heap on the planks, eyeing me pathetically. I whistled to mum, and struck steadily southward across Golden Ball Brow, for I dare not attempt to land again on Men-a-Vaur for fear of getting in the same mess again myself . . . on Northwethel islet just west of Teän I landed in a grassy bay and put him ashore in the thrift. He was perking up by now, and standing on his own feet. Half an hour later he was surrounded by crumbs that *Lugworm* sent across, and mum was strident overhead, so next day when I saw him trotting round the beach, I reckoned no harm done.

If you should have a mind to dream a while, you will not do better than to lie alone on the fernclad southern bank of Nornour and watch the evening sun set fire to the Eastern Isles, so russet and gold do they glow across the wine dark sea. Sit quiet here with me for a while and listen to the wind through the fern leaves. *Lugworm* is half asleep, playing with her own reflection, her two masts seeming to probe impossibly deep into the shallow sandy bay.

Ganilly is aflame, and beyond that Great Arthur and distant St Mary's take up the symphony of colour, echoing that other expression of an underlying music which is with you always on the islands: the song of the sea. It accompanies you

Top, Lugworm in Teän bay, low water. Hedge Rock on right and St. Mary's in background; *centre, Ben* gets a refit on Teän. Paintbrush is made from a piece of old rope!; *bottom,* 'Boat's in a dreadful state,' she said. *Lugworm* on Goats Point, St. Martin's isle

Top, Round island . . . calm; *centre,* Round island . . . storm; *bottom,* splicing the anchor warp in my bivouac after the gale on Teän

everywhere, like your own unconscious mind, and obeys the same law, manifesting itself only when the ever clamorous 'I' is unaware, bringing you nearer to reality than the barrier of sense experience allows.

Listen idly to that song, and you may hear the echoes of other times and other people who walked these isles when they had different contours to those you see now.

Legend has it that the isles were once joined to Cornwall, and romantic stories of a sunken continent of Lyonesse fire the imagination. More in the realm of fact, however, is the evidence available from fascinating archaeological finds throughout the group which indicate that comparatively recently either the level of the sea or the height of the land was somewhat different. There are also accounts of what appears to be a laid stone course on Crow Bar, suggesting that this was once a road linking St Martin's to St Mary's. Indeed, today the sea level would have to fall less than two metres and you could walk dryshod at low water spring tides from Cruthers Hill at the southern tip of St Martin's via Guthers Island and Crow Bar to St Mary's: a distance of one and a half miles. Even now it's possible at this state of tide to wade from St Martin's to Tresco.

Right below us, on the edge of the beach are the walls of small circular houses. It may well be that under those quivering and probing reflections of *Lugworm*'s masts are buried further homesteads, for certainly the upper reaches of the tide level have destroyed some of these strange buildings. What fashion of people were these, who lived in the small round houses huddled close together here on Nornour, their crude stone walls sheltered against the rising ground to the north and whose low narrow doors faced eastward away from the prevailing winds? The gales of 1962 laid their habitations bare, but the artefacts found within and around those habitations seem to have presented more of a mystery than they solve. The pottery suggests they were active in the pre-Roman Iron Age, and later reoccupied during the Roman period, since datable Roman coins, pottery of the time, and pipe-clay figurines have been found here. But the most remarkable finds were a collection of finely worked bronze brooches, some rings and bracelets, mostly dating to the second century A.D. which suggests either that this group was then the centre of a sophisticated metal-working culture, or perhaps the site of a shrine to which such ornaments might have been brought, or even a collection point at which the manufactured objects were completed for onward distribution elsewhere. Whatever the answer, in the houses you may still see traces of their way of life, for there are the hearths, the partition walls, and even pestles and mortars for grinding grain. But has the land fallen, or has the sea risen? Most probably the former, for it is known that the whole edge of this continental shelf has been subject to submergence even in recorded history.

It's fascinating to lie here on this warm slope and visualise the topography of those days. It may well be that at some time these islands were all one. In imagination the eye sweeps down a green valley which is now Crow Sound sloping seaward to the south. West of St Mary's hill, out through the great flat grassy plain of St Mary's Roads, one might see the glint of water where the broken outcrops of scattered isles which now form the western rocks finally capitulate to the sea. Northward the major spine of the isle curves through St Martin's, Teän, Tresco and Bryher, and afar, very distant, one may still hear the ever-present voice of the sea.

A small, green world with its own protective moat, supporting stock and growing cereals, whose population traded with, and occasionally doubtless united in defence against marauding pirates.

Certainly, when the Romans withdrew from southern Britain in the fifth century A.D., these isles formed a handy base for the marauders who then found the softened British an easy prey. Around 980 A.D. a marauding fleet of Norsemen – some hundred ships – came to the isles, led by the King of Norway, one Olaf Tryggvessön who, after the death of his wife, had fared forth in savage fury, harrying the shores of England, Ireland and Scotland, eventually arriving at the Scillies. This little bloodbath had apparently taken him some four years, if the somewhat confused history of the sagas is to be relied on. But it appears that he heard of a soothsayer on these isles who foretold the future. To him he sent a certain one of his henchmen who was like himself in appearance, instructing him to inform the soothsayer that he was

62

indeed the king and ask his fortune. The soothsayer, however, apparently saw through the ruse, sending him off with a flea in his ear and the instructions to stop fooling and remain true to his real king. This so impressed Olaf that he forthwith arranged to meet the wise man himself and being entirely human ask how he might yet increase his power.

Now this wise man was a Christian, and by means of a certain prophecy, persuaded the warlike Olaf that there was more to this Christianity than might at first meet the eye of a savage marauder from Scandinavia. To cut a long story short (and it's all laid down in the *Heimskringla*, which is one of the best known sagas of the old Norse kings) Olaf and all his gang were christened and stayed in the isles until the autumn, when they sailed for England, and eventually carried his new creed to Norway, Sweden, Denmark and Iceland, enforcing it in what was later to become a well exercised 'christian' manner – at the point of the sword!

So Christianity (Norse brand) may have found its way to Scandinavia from these isles, but the way of it sounds little to the credit of its founder, and one wonders, lying here looking at the peaceful beauty of earth, whether it's not a pity that the vehicle for the spread of man's religion has to be man himself!

So where were we? Lying peacefully on Nornour, with dear old Buggerlugs waiting patiently out there in the bay . . . then let's wander down through the round houses and bid adieu to the ghosts that undoubtedly haunt these shores, for south bay on Teän is a safer place to spend the night, and have we not our own hearth already shaped and blackened there waiting between the tidemarks on the rocks?

Chapter Three

Storm and Calm

But of course it wasn't always paradise. Dreamy days of sun there were in plenty, and lotus-eating on the lazy strands of Gugh, Bryher, Tresco . . . but in this life you have to take the smooth with the rough, and in *Lugworm* when it turns rough – it's rough!

I remember the following summer of '74. Who doesn't! I'd sailed *Lugworm* down again, arriving alone in the isles early July, and after that things grow a bit hazy for me, trying to isolate one soggy event from another. We seemed to spend our days desperately flitting from one isle to another for a lee, with the boat and all aboard becoming steadily more sodden. B. had stayed at home for a bit longer to set the spinach or something, and there were just the three of us again, *Ben, Lugworm* and I. Came one frightful night when, having escaped from a vicious southerly and gained the lee of Porth Conger between St Agnes and Gugh, three of the morning found a driving storm coming in from due north. It knocked up a sea that started breaking over *Lugworm*'s bow and it was all stops out to buoy and slip one anchor, weigh the other and beetle off to safety elsewhere before she foundered . . . and that was the pattern of it, with sleep becoming more and more at a premium and never a night but some elemental disaster foaming along to wash the dreams away.

Finally, we got ourselves jammed in Hottentot Bay for three days. For the first time I felt moderately safe and protected from every blessed quarter of the compass. In driving rain and to the honking of fascinated seals I spent a whole afternoon building a hideyhole of rocks, roofed over with *Ben*, suitably weighted. It was so cosy that evening with a bright bonfire keeping out the gloom that I moved all cooking gear ashore and set up house, Crusoe fashion, on that uninhabited isle. It was the best night yet, albeit hellish smoky, but there's a rare and primaeval satisfaction in listening to the howl of a gale and the venomous spit of rain on hot ashes – when you're snug and warm in the glow from a great driftwood fire! I decided to make it a permanent base until the weather changed.

Next day I swear the tide was the highest since Ararat. There must have been five tons of kelp jammed in my hidey-hole and Little Arthur itself needed waterwings. A drenching westerly, heavy with the scent of weed ripped from the Western Reefs, scorched in, tripped over Little Ganninick and in sheer spite kicked *Ben,* weights and all, up and into a bank of Hottentot figs. *Lugworm,* denuded now by the removal of tent and masts, did a tango from side to side of the bay with both anchors straining, and I stood shivering and miserable, with despair not very far up to weather.

It was the night after that on the phone that there came a faint note of alarm in B.'s voice: 'It looks pretty ghastly,' she said, 'because on the weather chart the Atlantic is covered in one big cobweb . . . and the man said there is a typhoon or something just west of the Shamrocks . . . DO take care, darling!'

'It'll come from the west,' I thought, scurrying off to the south shore of Teän . . . with one ear jammed to the transistor. We holed up near the ruined house, reckoning we could get as good a lee behind the Hedge rocks and all those reefs strewn about as anywhere else. September 7th it was, and I shall never forget it. I bedded *Lugworm* down on the beach two hours after high and hauled *Ben* on to the grass, clamping him down with a hundredweight or so of rocks, just for sure. The rain continued and the wind just for cussedness swung south and got into gear. At two-thirty in the morning, the tent was playing merry havoc and the boat all but sailing on dry land. I lay grimly listening to an ever-approaching roar as the tide crept back over Rascal's Ledge, foamed round the foot of Foreman's Isle and encircled the Hedge. The wind had a hysterical scream about it as though it were harbouring wild devils plucked from the hoary wastes of the Atlantic.

And so it was, a whole cargo of them shrieking and tearing at the sea ... it was horrifying! 'Hell and highwater,' I fumed. 'If this boat floats with the tent on her, we shall be awash!' And I ruminated, with sinking heart.

Oh yes, it's all very well to question why I wasn't already out and battening everything down for the fray, but at three in the morning there's a deal of inertia to be overcome 'ere one leaves a warm sleeping bag and walks out for a perishing gale to clap around the vitals! But, of course, it had to be done, and once more I moved all my gear ashore, piling it under one wall of the ruin, every last stitch of it this time – masts, bottomboards, tent and outboard. Even the stores and food to lighten ship. By five a.m. the surf was licking under her chin and the storm had by my reckoning reached force nine. With a lurch she finally lifted to the first wave. I leapt aboard and shortened in to pull her clear of the beach with two anchors out.

And there for two hours I bounced, skinned up like a yellow haggis with oilskins tight over three jerseys and long woollen combinations. It was impossible even to look up to weather: spray and wind would have clawed your eyes out. But sailors expect this sort of insult; what began to alarm me was a gradual but sickening deadness in the buoyant movement of *Lugworm*. She was growing heavy and unresponsive, and frantically in the dawn light I cast about for a cause. The bilges were moderately dry: I'd been baling since she floated. What could be the trouble?

I turned, shielding my eyes and tried to peer to weather. Aghast, I saw that half a haystack of weed was entangled round the two anchor warps, pulling the bow down with the dead weight of it. I lurched forward, scrabbling over the stem, and got a hogshead of sea in my face which knocked me back, for my added weight forward was putting her bow under. There was nothing else for it: over the side I had to go, and sharp, clawing at that slimy mass and just able to toe the bottom in the troughs. At that moment, with a small explosion, one anchor warp parted and there was *Lugworm* sheering away with me trailing behind like a sea-anchor. Riding now to one warp only, she began veering madly in a wide arc, swinging beam-on to the seas at each extremity and shipping them green over her gunwales. In desperation, and waiting the right moment, I reached up and slipped the second warp. Together we sheared across the bay and somewhere on the trip I managed to roll myself back aboard, only to leap out again to frantically guide her in to the lee shore at a point clear of rocks. And there, with each successive surge of the rising tide, she drove further back, until after high water the maelstrom started receding to leave her all fouled up with twisted masses of weed and heaped shingle. She was a forlorn sight, well above normal high water mark . . . but safe!

I made a bivouac under that wall with the boat's gear, while the wind shrieked from out of a demented sky, driving the rain horizontally. With the dawn – if you can call it that – far from abating, the fury increased. Only later did I learn that a full hurricane had again passed across the islands during those traumatic hours. But the wind had now veered to the west, and was still veering to bring horrible grey scud, ripped and stranded at the edges, bansheeing over Teän. All that day I tried to get a fire going, but there was no dry wood . . . At evening, after a makeshift meal and with coming darkness, I wrapped myself in the tent and huddled close to the wall on a platform of driftwood. Sometime in the night I woke with an uneasy feeling and, switching on the torch, caught a ring of bright shining eyes before they receded smartly into the bracken: island rats, the sweetest little things come to keep me company and clean up my scraps.

With the dawn, cramped and stiff with cold, I opened my eyes – and shut them again instantly. Incredulously I slowly parted my lids again, praying I was having a nightmare . . . but it was still there, an inch or two from my nose and observing it closely . . . a black, wonderfully articulated scorpion!

Now I know perfectly well you just don't come across scorpions in England, much less paddling about in seaboots in a driving force 12, but I've seen these things often in Greece and this little fellow was of close enough resemblance for me to give it the full benefit of any doubt. As it dug its clawed feet into the tent and raised that tail ominously up and over, staring me in the eyes as brazen as you please, my heart all but stopped. I have a firmly held conviction about instant death: it should be avoided at all cost!

But how?

With every guarded twitch of mine that tail twitched up and over in response. Still as a corpse already, I stared back at the frightful thing and went cold as a fish. At such moments, strange fantasies flit through the mind. Scorpion . . . Scorpio . . . dammit I was born on November 13th and my guiding constellation is the heavenly SCORPIO! Was this grievous moment, perhaps, all predestined from my very first howl! Was the symbol of all that motivated me eventually to pitch me back into the limbo of Erebus. Then something began vibrating in the soundbox of my mind. 'Try telepathy,' it said . . . 'TRY TELEPATHY!'

I took my eyes off that pregnant arched tail, looked the creature square on the nose and soundlessly sent out thoughts of . . . FRIENDSHIP? 'Friend!' I willed. Slowly it cocked its lovely little head on one side and – I swear it – raised a curious eyebrow. Agonisingly slowly the tail sank back down and the urgency drifted away. Things were at a point where, with utmost caution and no quick movement whatever, I could draw up one arm and grip the fold of the tent below my right ear. Quick as thought I ripped it back and away, trapping the thing beneath its layers, and jumped clear, staggering through the pile of boat gear in my panic. Then, carefully, I dragged the tent clear of the wall and unfolded it with a stick. There he was the little devil, shaking himself and all of a spite at the turn of things. Again we faced each other but this time I was standing with stick in hand, and the situation was reversed. I raised the stick and took aim . . .

But then a strange thing happened. Seeing him standing there so small, with tail raised in fierce but helpless defiance, I suddenly no longer wanted to bring down that stick. 'Somewhere,' I found myself thinking, 'back in that wall, there'll be another little fellow like you, to whom you're both the beginning and the end of things and entirely cuddleable. We're both just making the best of a bad job and all we wanted was a bit of warmth. You could have bowled me out easy as licking your lips backalong . . . but you didn't.'

I put him gently on the end of the stick and laughed as he

scuttled deep into a crack in the wall a bit further along. I felt a prize fool, but a bit shaken for all that.

It was the following morning I got the telegram in St Mary's. 'Arriving Noon Thursday. Miss you. B.'

'Look cuckoo,' I explained desperately over the telephone that evening, dripping in oilskins. 'This is just no place for a girl . . . we're fighting for survival. Honestly, the three of us are beginning to sag round the edges. You'll die of exposure!'

'Nonsense,' came the voice. 'It's a bit windy, that's all. You obviously need me, you're losing your buoyancy . . . it's Brymon Airways, quarter to twelve at the airport. I love you . . .'

You won't believe me, but even as that monoplane wobbled in to the greensward the heavens parted their ashen lips and smiled. For the sheer joy of feeling hot sunshine and a warm drying wind I insisted on walking back to Hugh Town from the 'drome. 'I knew it,' she said, radiant in summer frock, it's just your state of mind – you needed me!'

Well, in the circumstances you don't argue, do you? What's the point when the sun is so hot it's bikinis and parasols and us ghosting under genoa and a kiss of warm wind back up to Teän. Only half of me wanted to spit! We even caught a thumping great pollack on the way and baked it on the rocks for supper. Next day was brisk, sunny, and obviously sent for drying-out. We bedded on that lovely warm sand at Goats Point, St Martin's, and she stretched everything in the boat along our anchor warp with crossed oars as a clothes prop. 'You've let things get out of hand,' she said, 'the boat's in a dreadful state!' I just looked at the barometer and boiled quietly.

It went on like that for a week. We met up with friends and spent dreamlike days toasting in the tussocks on Samson, Bryher, Great Arthur and Teän. We caught fish and buckets full of shrimps, cooking them on deserted beaches with *Ben* propped up to keep the late summer sun off delicately pinking hides . . . can you believe it! There were langorous teas of stewed blackberries topped with that delicious thick cream from the island Jersey cows . . . and we turned lobster red and laughed and lived like Adam and Eve in Eden.

70

The isle of Annet was our paradise during that fortnight she was with me. We used to spend the nights in Porth Conger on St Agnes – a handy berth this since at high water; in the event of the wind going north, *Lugworm*, with an inch and a gulp to spare, can skim across the top of the sandy spit that joins the isle to Gugh.

After a lazy breakfast, we'd sail over to what we called Rocky Bay on the north-east shore of Annet. It's a foul place to find yourself on a lee shore, but the trick is to reach quickly the mile across to Pereglis Bay on St Agnes if the weather begins to deteriorate. We would leave the mizzen up in *Lugworm* while she was at anchor, and the west wind would keep her streaming away from the shore and safe off the rocks.

It's hilarious, B. and I in *Ben* together. *Ben*'s not intended for two, and B., as I've said, is slim and tall. She has to entwine her long legs with mine and keep her centre of gravity down low as possible while dodging the flailing inboard ends of the oars. One false move and we're towing *Ben*, who seems to enjoy it all as much as we do. I leap out while we're still afloat, for one foul contact with a rock and *Ben* is punctured. It's a bit of a technique, that leap, for soon as my own weight is gone, up *Ben* will tip and pitch B. in backwards over the stern! So we worked out a method. At the moment I leap over the side (there can be no half measures, you're either in or out of *Ben* with no dilly-dallying) and find a footing, B. slides forward from the stern to the centre of the skiff. I then hold *Ben* steady until she has disembarked too. It all works very well provided I get a firm footing straight away, but it's not always easy on rounded slimy boulders!

Annet is beautiful. Like most of the isles there is no vestige of trees, but it's carpeted with thick clumps of thrift, sprouting from a deep springy green carpet of grass, through which burst great shoulders of sparkling granite. It is the haunt of blackbacks, and their clamour when we arrive is often disturbing, since they have a habit of soaring up, then diving to within a few inches of one's head before spreading their wings and swooping off again. After a bit they get used to us though, and the great thing is not to disturb them too much, remembering it's THEIR isle, and we who are the intruders.

We spent days there, searching the pebble beaches and hum-mocky rises to identify the wild plants. There is sea holly to be found, its blue flowers like thistles in late August, but it is becoming rare, and on no account should be picked. Curled dock sprouts in profusion between the pebbles, and scentless mayweed with its little white daisylike flowers turns the top of the shoreline into a fringe of white lace before the thrift and fern take over.

But these western isles, so far as I am concerned, are unique for their magical rock pools. At low water springs, there is a fantasy world of colour and form to be found in the trans-lucent depths of those pools. I have hundreds of colour trans-parencies, taken through the water, of the myriad formed weeds and sea anemones. We would select some soft springy turf bank on the western shore and spend the days basking in the sun. Both of us were already tanned the colour of mahogany, and still the weather held, for that most blessed fortnight that B. was with us. Out to the west the Bishop's Rock light stood slim against the sky, and all around the apparently calm face of the sea would suddenly gape into stretches of white spume where the Tearing Ledges, Retarrier, Gilstone, Crim and Gunners reefs broke surface.

Often, as B. and I stretched there in the grass gazing across those lazy sunsoaked miles of sea, there came over us a strange sense of privilege – privilege at being able to view it all from a situation of calm and complete safety, when the beauty of it was our sole concern.

'Can you begin to imagine that disastrous night nearly two hundred and seventy years ago?' I asked her. 'Do you ever get the feeling that the sea, as we're seeing it now from this tiny islet, is somehow oddly predatory – waiting its time, sleep-ing with one eye just open, watching its chance . . .'

'Have you any idea how it came about?' she replied.

'Only what I've read, but knowledge of the sea and one's own experience and imagination can pretty accurately fill in the details. It's all fairly well recorded. One thousand four hundred men lost their lives that night of 22nd October 1707 between Gilstone and Crim – out there, where it's breaking now.'

A line of distant white water – the thinnest etching of snow on a vast canvas of hazy smoke blue – silently appeared, slowly extended, then merged back into nothingness. No sound was there, but I knew that, had we been on the reef at that moment, the power of it would have pulverised us.

He was fifty-seven years old, Sir Cloudesley Shovel, the Commander-in-Chief in his Flagship *Association*, a second-rater of the line, 1,459 tons, 90 guns and crewed by 680 men. In April of that year his fleet had taken part in the bombard-ment of Toulon, and twenty-one ships were returning to Ports-mouth on a voyage which was at first beset by continuous bad weather. Conditions improved, but evidently not enough for them to establish their exact latitude, and longitude was always a difficult problem in those days before they had really accurate clocks. At any rate, they were in general doubt, and he ordered his fleet to heave-to sometime during the day of 21st October in order to take soundings. You must remember that at that time a ship had but one method of doing this : to lower a line down with a heavy lead 'armed' at its bottom with a pad of wax. The mariner noted the depth on feeling the lead hit the bottom, and an examination of the wax often revealed the nature of the seabed. Sand, shingle, mud, or whatever, would be a clue to the general area and, of course, the depth itself was a good guide to one's position, for the charts gave some information about depths even in those days.

Of course, really accurate soundings could be carried out only when the vessel was stopped, otherwise the lead and line tended to stream aft, making it appear deeper than in truth it was. You can imagine the fleet, after weeks at sea, on that grey overcast day, closing one another and drifting with sails aback while each took an independent sounding. It's more than likely that boats would then be lowered for a conference aboard the flagship, since quite clearly the Admiral was very worried about his exact position.

If so, it would indicate also that the sea conditions were not all that bad, for you can't send away boats in anything of a storm.

The result of the decision then made was the worst peace-time disaster in Britain's maritime history. Incredible though it may seem, they came to the conclusion that the fleet was somewhere off Ushant. But remember they had sailed well over a thousand miles since coming through the Straits of Gibraltar. Almost certainly they would have made a landfall to fix their position at Cape St Vincent on the southern tip of Portugal and would take a departure from Cape Finisterre before crossing the Bay of Biscay. It would be only reasonable that any mariner of the time would seek to gain a landfall again at Ushant to establish his position before running up the Channel, and if one has this objective in mind, it's difficult to jettison the idea that one is not within ten or twenty miles of your intended position. One thing would be obvious: they could not be east of Ushant, otherwise they would have been getting signs of the coast of France, and the bottom shallowing up. In fact, their reckoning was some hundred miles out, for they were close south-west of these Scilly Isles. The weather, as night came in, began to worsen again.

There is a story, and I think it very likely true, that a crew member of one of the ships was himself a Scillonian. This man, it's stated, somehow sensed by the look of the sea, and the smell of it, that he was in home waters. He is reputed to have insisted on conveying his opinion to the Admiral, but was overruled by the more weighty views of the navigators. Admiral Shovel set course before that rising wind, as he thought, to enter the English Channel – and ran the whole fleet straight into the thick of the islands!

What is amazing is that of the twenty-one ships, only five were actually wrecked. *Association*, striking the Gilstone Ledges, fired three guns in an attempt to warn the others before sinking in 90 feet of water. *Romney*, a 48-gun ship-of-the-line, struck the Crebininicks and went down. Only one of her 280 hands, the quartermaster George Lawrence from Hull, survived by clinging to the rocks. Crim claimed the *Eagle*, with all four hundred and forty crew drowned. The *Firebrand*, of eight guns, struck the Gilstone Ledge, floated off but went down while trying to make St Agnes. The *Phoenix*, a fireship, struck the reefs but managed to beach on Tresco and was later salvaged.

It may be that the remainder of the fleet, in the gathering dark and increasing wind, had become somewhat scattered, choosing not to lie too close to one another in the poor

74

visibility. At any rate some of them passed north and south of the Isles, while one or two appear to have miraculously passed straight through the inter-island channels and clear out the other side.

Account has it that Sir Cloudesley himself took to his barge with his treasure chest and a pet greyhound, as the *Association* foundered, and this again argues that the sea conditions were not impossibly violent. It may well be, however, that as a result of the recent bad weather to the south, there was a big swell running and that would account for the dreadful toll once the craft had actually struck the reefs. At any rate, the Admiral is said to then have been wrecked a second time on the beach at Porth Hellick, St Mary's Isle, and to this day there is a monument there on the spot where he was first buried. He was later disinterred and reburied in Westminster Abbey.

And now a truly grim tale emerges. It is said that many years after the fateful night an island woman, when on her deathbed, told how she had found the Admiral still alive on the beach and completely exhausted. Seeing two rings on his fingers, she confessed to murdering the poor wretch – a task that was all too easy I imagine in his defenceless situation – and removing the rings. She produced one of them, set with an emerald, which she had been afraid to sell in case such an easily identifiable object be traced to her. The tale has it that when the Admiral's body was found, there were indeed the marks of two rings on his fingers, but no sign of the rings themselves. The woman felt that by confessing this act she would in some way absolve herself from guilt.

The sea sighed quietly at our feet. Southward the bleak brown slab of Melledgan broke the horizon, Gorregan, Daisy, Rosevear and Crebawethan pushed their white-coated tips up from the depths, and behind Crebawethan towered the slim pencil of Bishop's Rock Lighthouse.

'The Bishop wasn't there in those days,' I added. 'But it's odd that they didn't see the brazier kept lit on St Agnes lighthouse. Visibility must have been very poor.'

'Surely, they would have heard the breakers on the reefs. Wouldn't that have warned them in time?' B. queried.

I put myself in imagination out there, in pitch black of

night, with the wind singing through the rigging, and that agony of doubt born of not knowing with certainty one's exact position. There must have been greater alertness operating among the officers and men, for in such a situation only a fool is off his guard, and those men were not fools.

'Almost certainly they were running before the rising wind,' I mused, 'possibly with breaking seas alongside, which make a great deal of sound. You don't hear the roar of surf when its downwind of you, not with other sounds close in your ears. You don't even see it when you're looking over the backs of the breakers until you're right on them. Maybe a cable or so off they realised their error. But what could they do with those ships, unmanoeuvrable as they were, incapable of beating to windward, and sluggish in response to the helm? They hadn't a chance.'

But these were grim thoughts for a tranquil sunladen autumn afternoon, so we put them from our minds, wandered across to *Ben* on the eastern shore and brought from *Lugworm* the two mackerel we'd caught that morning and some bread, potatoes and drink.

Is there anything to match the peace of sitting close to a driftwood fire on a lonely beach, while the sun bids adieu to the day, and all those scents that come with the evening drift up from the warm grass and bracken close about. I remember we crushed some samphire in our hands and inhaled its clean fresh pungence, a scent which, for me, will always evoke the joy of solitude and freedom on lonely rockstrewn shores.

We grilled the mackerel, baked the potatoes in their jackets and wrapped in tinfoil among the red embers of the fire, and rounded the meal off with a bottle of Blue Nun, watching while the isle drew in her skirts as the tide encroached. Rock pools – liquid lakes of light – merged back into the mother ocean and the light continued to fade. *Lugworm* took us quietly back to Porth Conger, running goosewinged gently through the channel between Teneers Ledge and Browarth, rounding up beneath the inn there atop the slipway, and the bay held us safe all night.

September crept out, and B. returned home. Apart from the odd visit to St Mary's to provision and water ship I drifted deeper and deeper into a pattern of happy indolence. Ye gods, what days those isles have given me! Solitude is essential for a writer, but on occasions she can be a misleading mistress who weaves a spell around the soul and drugs the mind. Indeed it must be so, for why else would a chap begin to spend contented hours, days and finally weeks alone just listening . . . to silence?

Baked by days of languid sun the bracken had long since turned gold while I, alone in my kingdom, tanned to a matching brown. We would make occasional sorties, *Lugworm*, *Ben* and I, from Teän down to those Western Isles, anchoring between St Agnes and Gugh for a night or two before ghosting back round Samson and Bryher. We explored all those offlying islets, always finding a safe night billet under a craggy lee. With bow and stern warp looped over a pinnacle of rock we would jam ourselves in some ridiculous gulley where no real yacht dare ever venture. But always we returned thankfully to the sheltered solitude of Teän.

Meanwhile, summer was ageing, her weather turning grey. I remember one October dawn as the first breath of a sea-fret just dampened the scarred face of Ganilly, we crept past Guthers, hand-in-hand with the ebb. Its huge rocky Dodo peered watchful through the mist and Tobaccoman's rocks chuckled and swirled close aboard as we cleared away south of the ill-famed Minalto ledges, for I had a mind to explore those savage western rocks at close quarters. We reached down under a grey sky between St Agnes and Annet, awestruck at the unbelievable fangs in Hellweathers Neck rearing up to rip and tear at the low cloud. As Melledgan – scarce more than a whitened perch for a hundred and more cormorants – fell away astern it was as if the sea and the rocks closed in; very different to those sunsoaked days I had spent there with B. Suddenly the safe world of Man was gone: we were three unwanted intruders in an alien, desolate wintry place.

It was then I saw the seal. Old, grey, disfigured by wounds and scars, he watched us from a ledge and there was no love in his eye. I stared at him and he stared back at me. As the muted thunder of swell from the distant reefs whispered in my ears it was as if, from the deep soundings of memory there came welling up a strange, disturbing warning. That

old warrior became the very embodiment of a verse written
long ago . . .

> *One alone . . . all alone . . . wary of ear and eye.*
> *The western wind and the sea's my home — Lord of the*
> * Reefs am I!*
> *Well you may stare, you human thing, my world here once*
> * was yours.*
> *But what part of you now knows the lonely wind that sings*
> * on these barren shores?*
> *You have forgot the twilight deep where the kelpen forests*
> * flow . . .*
> *Where the long slow breath of the ocean gives life to a*
> * world below.*
> *Be gone with your boat, you human being — best let*
> * those memories die.*
> *You bring the scent of an unreal thing—*
> *One with the Sea am I!*

So we stood off, *Lugworm, Ben Gunn* and I, and set course
back to our soft, safe world of home, for we knew that, all
unsuspecting, we had stirred memories best forgotten. They
flowed too deep, and too powerfully, for this thin veneer,
which is the armour of twentieth-century man, to withstand.

Chapter Four

Ensay

We were stalking mussels, a friend and I on the shore at Rock back in the spring of 1975, when I mentioned that a Cornish seaside resort is no place for a writer in the high season. 'In a sense,' I told him, triumphantly cornering a *mytilus edulus*, 'a writer is always working. As long as he's still warm he's manipulating the bricks of his trade . . . ideas. But it doesn't look that way to others and you catch envious comments when folk see you more or less permanently denizened in the boat, the sun, and the water. They're right, of course, in a way,' I continued. 'But when the tools of your trade lie in a ream of paper, a portable typewriter, and what goes on between your two ears, only a fool wouldn't take advantage of the freedom it allows.'

'But that's only the visible side of it,' I hammered away at him (he was that sort of friend). 'There are the sleepless nights, the agonised hours of searching for just the right construction to convey an atmosphere – so as not to overdo it and end with purple passages – and yet avoid a dreary record of facts.'

He listened for a while, then told me to pipe down, for, as he pointed out, 'You're disturbing the peace of the morning. But if that's really how you feel why don't you drop a line to my brother who's doctoring in Africa. He's got a crumbling old mansion on an uninhabited isle by the name of Ensay, somewhere in the Outer Hebrides. He might lend it to you . . . there'd be nothing but you and the whelks, and they're not loquacious!'

The itch started from that moment. I suppose if you live in the extreme south west of Cornwall it's only human nature

79

that sooner or later you'll develop an itch to putter off to the far-flung extremities of Scotland – just to see if the other man's sea is bluer, so to speak! I scratched the itch a bit that evening with B., taking a few soundings as it were, and found it a bit deep for throwing out an anchor. But it's astonishing what a word here, a suggestion there, can do to the psychology of a woman. After a week or so she was practically begging me to be off and leave her in peace. Opportunity, they say, knocks but once.

By the end of April, a friend and I had the trip more or less organised and open-ended so far as time was concerned. Trevor, who is mad as I am myself, volunteered to tow *Lugworm* as far as Hadrian's Wall and I knew he wouldn't be hard-hearted enough to just leave us there drooping by the roadside. Which is why at this moment we're sitting on a draughty quay wall in the sleet at Leverburgh, with little else but sea and sky out there in the Sound of Harris and the grey ghost of the isle of Ensay eyeing us through the gale. Leverburgh is the modern name for Obbe, by which name the village was known prior to the Lord Leverhulme fiasco, which is another story.

There are one thousand two hundred miles more on the clock than when we left Rock five days ago. I got lost three times somewhere in the blizzardy peaks of those Scottish Highlands while Trev was asleep, and we both passed thoughts with a ferry which didn't (and accounts for the excessive mileage). But here we are clutching a sprig of heather and a bottle of the 'guid stuff', and it looks as though we'll be needing it from the strained look of the barometer.

'Uncle's away on the isle,' said the rosy-faced youngster back in the village. 'He's been there this fortnight lambing, but he's expecting you and will have the lambs out of the oven before you arrive.' We put it down to an endearing Gaelic turn of phrase.

Southward, the dark silhouette of North Uist all but hides Hecla's two thousand foot peak towering up behind, and there's snow on its icy pate. A shivering north-easter is elbowing its way down the Minch, bouncing off Lewis and Skye to howl onward with hysterical Norse-filled fury to freeze all you pappy unsuspecting southerners. Nothing remains twixt us

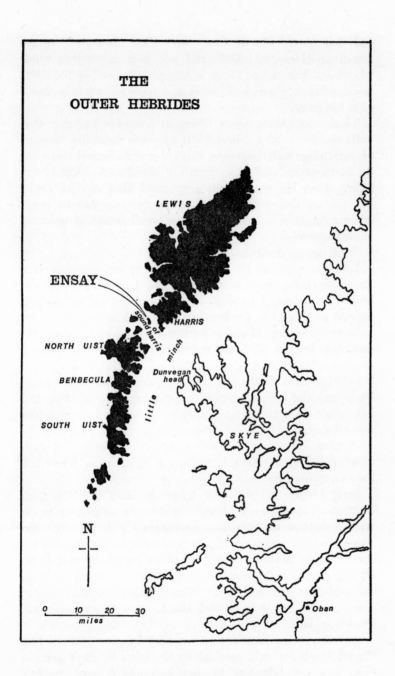

THE
OUTER HEBRIDES

LEWIS

ENSAY

HARRIS

sound of harris

minch

NORTH UIST

BENBECULA

Dunvegan head

little

SOUTH UIST

SKYE

N

0   10   20   30
miles

Oban

and that lonely isle of Ensay save these 'Narrows', as the
Sound of Harris is called – and one look across that wind-
whipped streak of turbulence is enough! Scoured by the sleet-
laden wind it glares back at us and there's a steely warning
glitter in its eye.

There's something about living in a car for five days that
dulls the brain of a sailor. Next morning came the moment
of launching, with *Lugworm* checked and rechecked and even
the north-easter holding its breath in anticipation. Now Leverhulme, bless his ghost, built a splendid little slipway, down
one side of the pier at Obbe, and everything was set ready
when a haggis-filled voice from the small crowd of watchers
offered sage advice:

'Ye'll noo git doon tha!'

I looked again at the slipway. True, it was certainly very
steep and there was an unaccountable kink halfway down.
Maybe he's right, I ruminated: if things got out of control,
happen we'd be O.K. for firewood next week or so.

'Best gie along Macusbic's place doon o'er the shingles,'
came another broad Scots voice, and many hands pointed
along a gravel track. I'm a great believer in heeding local
knowledge as a matter of principle, even when it's wrong.
Back into the car we hopped and were scarcely in second
gear when there came a soul-deflating judder and a report like
a pistol shot.

'You've left the jockey wheel down!' we brayed at each
other in self-exoneration . . . but not a bit of it, we'd just left
the mizzen mast up!

Now I must tell you that telephone lines in Obbe span
quite colossal distances between posts – it's something to do
with a shortage of trees in these barren highlands – with the
result that the wires sag more than a bit in the middle. So
there was my mizzen snapped off like a carrot and half Obbe
off the 'phone, and I won't voice the Gaelic thoughts on these
dammed furriners with their boats! Though mark you, not
one critical word was uttered aloud, so well mannered are
these braw lads.

Anyway, by the time that lot was sorted out and I'd climbed
the telegraph post and married up the wires by sheer inspira-
tion, that ebb tide was looking lean and hungry. In fact

Macusbic's slipway already ended short and there was a sort of moist Gobi desert of rocks between it and the still receding water. But there were also eight willing pairs of hands at the ready – it's astonishing how folk appear when there's a novelty like us around – so we man-handled all 1,200 lb. of laden *Lugworm* across an improvised ramp of pitprops. And there we were at last – afloat!

We could see the gable-ends of *home*, snug at the head of a perfect little sandy bay over there on the isle of Ensay two miles off, and together we pored over the chart. 'Ye'll mind that spring tide, noo,' one of the helpers shouted. 'She'll be flowing eastward into the Minch come the flood, and westward to the Atlantic come the ebb, give or take a dram.' I looked again across that steel-blue strip of insulation. Part of it appeared to be flowing eastward and the rest undoubtedly flowing westward! Which dram did we give . . . and more to the point, which dram did we take. Then, as I watched, I swear my hair stood on end. Out there between the fangs of reefs that were already smelling the ozone, some two acres of kelp-smothered bottom rose from the water, sniffed, and gently sank out of sight again!

Of course, it did nothing of the sort: it was just a long, uneasy Atlantic swell funnelling down between Taobh Deas head and Pabbay Isle to heave its way through this bottleneck, and I thanked it for the timely warning and studied the chart with yet more dedication.

We beached *Lugworm* on that white sand of Ensay in front of the solitary old mansion and offloaded six months' supply of groceries and toilet rolls. It was a frolic, I can tell you, for there was a surge up and down that foreshore that boded ill should heaven start sneezing: what's more *Lugworm* had that feel about her that told me she was far from happy. We had left *Ben* at Rock out of sheer necessity, so had no tender – which precluded anchoring off.

There was no sign of John Mackenzie the farmer, but every sign of his charges: between us and the porch stood about a ton of jet-black Angus bull.

We stood at the top of a flight of concrete steps that led up from the beach, with a rusty iron gate between us and him, eyeing each other warily.

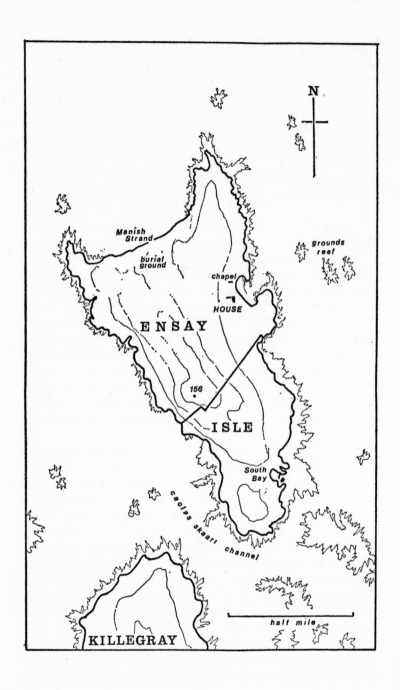

'Nip behind him and open the front door,' I instructed Trev. 'I'll distract his attention from here.' But that didn't work.

'I've got a better idea,' he volunteered. 'I'll work round the corner of the house, under that rainwater tank, and 'moo'. I'm very good at mooing: when he comes to court me I can nip through that gate into the other field and you open the door.' So it was arranged.

Trev crept along the beach, round the end of a lovely old castellated sea-wall, and positioned himself beside the water tank.

I thought he gave a good imitation of an enthusiastic cow. Angus blinked, hoofed up a yard or so of turf, and stomped off in the opposite direction. We waited until his indignant backside had disappeared round a barn and sprinted for the porch. The doors were jammed, but evidently unlocked. We put our shoulders to them and shoved.

On the peeling green walls of a hallway hung the colossal stuffed head of a water buffalo, or steer, or something with two horns that could have shishkebabbed six matadors and looked around for more. Its glass eyes blinked as the doors swung back, and a little shower of dust fell off its nose. There was a gaping hole in the plaster beneath him which left the horrid impression that he was given to moments of frustration, hanging about up there.

We slammed the doors behind us to safeguard our rear, and edged into the cavernous belly of the house.

'Anyone there?' I roared. The echo reverberated through the place and another cascade of dust came down off the nose. Not a sound. A door to our left led into a large front drawing room with bay window. There was an upright piano against one wall, and a spinning wheel beside it. Both appeared to be covered in snow. Above them, the white skull of a curly-horned ram grinned uncannily at us, and above that, a gaping hole in the plaster ceiling revealed a row of laths for all the world like the skeletal ribs of the old house, which accounted for the white dust.

Altogether the impression was macabre.

We crept along a dark passage, its walls peeling with a hideous yellow paper, and pushed gently on a dark brown

85

stained door. A massive kitchen, large enough for a castle and spare, complete with slate floor, a bare wooden table, a china sink that could have bathed Angus himself and a Rayburn stove. Something moved near the stove. I edged across to peer down in the half light ... and a querulous 'baa ...' brought me up all standing. There in the oven, just about as new as it could be, was the sweetest little wobble-legged lamb curled up. I felt the stove. 'He's not for dinner anyway, that's for sure,' I remarked to Trev, 'for the oven's little more than luke warm.'

There was a jacket hanging on a wall hook, and a pair of wellington boots under the sink. Signs of a meal were on the table, set for two. So we went exploring. Two doors led from the kitchen, one into a tiny courtyard which had evidently at some time been an extension of the house, for there was the ruin of an open fireplace in one wall. Another door led out to a beautifully protected lawn, overgrown now with weeds and thistles, but the grass cropped short by the sheep which were free-roaming all about the isle.

A wide staircase led up from the cavernous hall to the upper rooms. High on the wall, halfway up, hung another motheaten head, this time of an unfortunate antlered stag with the legend 'Alladale 1919' on a plaque beneath. A massive branding iron hung beside. There were four small bedrooms, the ceiling plaster down in all of them, and one huge, truly baronial room with a faded green carpet and a magnificent Scandinavian Jotul wood-burning stove fitted into what had been an open fireplace. A colossal – but sadly cracked – wall mirror hung above the mantelpiece. The ceiling of this room was intact, albeit badly cracked. Two iron bedsteads, with mattresses, stood against one wall.

But the view! One tall window looked north-east across the Sound to Roneval, 1,200 ft., another gazed south-west down half the length of the isle. Through this latter window we could see a greenswarded low headland – Borosdale as we came to know it – and beyond that, across a steel-blue strip of sea, the distant smoke blue hills of Skye. It was magnificent.

'This is the room for me,' I told Trev. 'It must have been the Laird's bedroom – but I wonder what's in all those outbuildings.' Beyond the outbuildings we could see more roofless ruins. Obviously at one time this had been a large homestead with all the supporting paraphernalia of a farm. There was something odd about the island slopes, though; they were uniformly ridged into long furrows, like wide, flat potato clamps, but smooth and rounded with the short-cropped grass. Wherever there was grass, the land was furrowed in this peculiar way.

Trevor was ferreting about somewhere in the bowels of the place, and I joined him in an upstairs storeroom. Against one wall hung a large, wide-brimmed coolie hat and a pair of white rubber armpit-high waders. There was a jumble of bric-à-brac, a wondrous great salmon-poaching pan a yard in length, a baby's playpen of canvas filled with tins of paint, two ship's bells and a miscellany of paraffin pressure lamps. In the centre of the room was a colossal wicker laundry basket containing two sets of brand new woven blue and green curtains. There were also five cases of blankets. The whole house was incredibly dry.

We set to carrying all our gear from the boat into the hallway, and in the middle of this heard voices back in the kitchen.

'Hullo there!' came a call, and John, gentleman, farmer, character, stomped down the corridor with hand extended. Odd, isn't it, how you take to some people instantly without the need of talking or introductions. Blue-eyes twinkled in a ruddy face. White hair, a chest like a barrel, short and stocky, wearing a dilapidated windcheater and corduroy trousers stuffed into wellingtons. 'We saw your boat on the beach from Borosdale. But we didn't really think you'd come across today – there's a sea running in the bay that'll pound her at high water. You'd best keep her down to the slip on the south side; she'll be safer there. Have ye had a meal? We've got half a sheep in the pot that'll be ready soon . . . come and meet Neil.'

Neil, a youth of some twenty or so years is John's son. Blond, tall, quiet and a little shy with strangers, we found him suckling the lamb from a rubber-teated bottle filled with warm milk. There was another lamb wobbling about under the table. 'Mother's dead,' he said . . . and that from Neil was a speech. In the corner of the kitchen, adjacent to the rayburn, was a two-burner bottled gas stove, and before half an hour was up there was the finest lamb stew, with turnip, pearl barley, onion and a few Gaelic herbs steaming up from four soup bowls, displayed about the central bottle of the 'guid stuff'.

We learned a great deal in a short time from John. Those peculiar furrows on the face of the isle, for instance. 'Lazy-beds,' he told us. 'When this house was the homestead, back at the turn of the century, there were some forty people lived on the isle: servants and farmhands. Soil hereabouts is at a premium, there's but a thin sprinkling of earth above the rock. They had to scrape what earth there was into long ridges to get the necessary depth leaving drainage furrows in between. Seaweed and sand was collected from the shore and mulched into this to bind and form humus. This was the way that the peaty deposits of the Highlands were turned into soil. Once drained by the furrows, the lime in the sand counteracted the acidity of the peat.'

'But why lazybeds?' I queried. It seemed a singularly inappropriate name.

'That I can't tell you,' he grinned. 'Maybe it was a sort of joke, for it must have been damned hard labour!

The isle was two miles in length and little more than a mile broad. Trevor and I spent next day, in a searing wind, walking its perimeter to get the scent of it all, and from that moment on I was bewitched. Maybe I'm a loner by nature, but if I had been asked to conjure up an idea of perfect bliss, why, I'd describe an isle covered in the greenest daisystrewn grass you can imagine, with sparkling bluffs of rocky gneiss pushing up through the sward to offer warm sundrenched grottoes from the winds . . . with a quarter of a mile of golden strand at one end, the dunes of which dropped sheer thirty feet and more to the edge of the surf-thundering beach. I'd have lambs frolicking all about, and fat contented cows drifting like ancient fleets of ships according to the weather. I'd have a rocky southern shore, with gullies and clefts to harbour the wild cormorants and seabirds, and the constant cries of the gulls in one's ears, and the lapwings, oystercatchers and red-shanks.

There would be a small semicircular sandy bay, with a

house at its head so old and full of character that it breathed history, and ages of work and love of the land, success and disaster . . . and the whole set in a sea so blue you'd think you were in the Ionian, with islands dotted like jewels all around for the exploring, for, of course, in this dream I'd have *Lugworm* at a mooring in the house bay, and just enough water – two miles of it – separating the isle from the nearest inhabited land from which provisions could be ferried. And Peace! There would be no sound of cars, nor jet planes carving up the silence with their obtrusive hysteria. Put me there, and I'd be in Paradise. Put me there, and I'd be on Ensay.

I just couldn't believe it.

Two days after we arrived, Trevor, John and Neil disembarked, for John's brother Donald came forging across from Obbe to fetch them in his thirty-foot power launch. He brought her to anchor in the bay and pulled ashore in a heavy clinker dinghy. With him came Alan, John's other son – wild-eyed with hair flying and a bandolier of twelve-bore cartridges strapped round his waist, a double-barrelled gun across his shoulders. 'Are they here yet?' came his urgent call even before the dinghy grounded. It was nonplussing. 'Are what here yet?' I queried, grabbing the painter and hauling the skiff up with the surge. 'The geese, man, the geese . . . are the greylags here?' John said something in Gaelic and from the look on Alan's face I knew the greylags hadn't arrived yet, for the

light seemed to have gone out of his life. 'Ah, well,' he said despondently, 'they'll maybe have arrived next time I'm home.'

But John was bringing all their gear from the house to the beach, and called me in for a conference. 'These now,' he pronounced, holding up a length of rusty chain from which hung a string of massive keys. 'Ye'll be wanting this one,' he said, selecting a small crowbar with flukes at one end. 'It's the key to the front porch, but maybe ye'll not be using that entrance much . . . it needs persuasion. This is for the back kitchen door, and there's the pantry cupboard, the dining room, the storeroom upstairs – that must be kept locked for it holds all the Doctor's island clothes and gear. And doubtless,' he continued with a slight but significant pause, 'ye'll be wanting this – the key to the barn.'

It seemed unlikely that I would want anything from the barn, but time would doubtless tell. In the meantime I thanked him, shook hands all round, bid adieu to Trevor with grateful thanks for all his effort on my behalf – and watched as the heavy-laden skiff was rowed off to the launch.

'Leave the tap in the scullery running,' John shouted as they climbed aboard. 'Spring water's best on the move and it keeps the pipe clear. Buttercup's due to calve so we'll be across in a week or two just to see everything's fine. Just light a fire on Borosdale if you break a leg or anything . . . happen we'll see it after dark.'

I watched them disappear through the outer rim of rocks protecting the southern end of the bay, then listened to the fading throb of the boat's engine as it probed out into the Sound. . . and I was alone.

King of all I surveyed.

Three days it took me to wash down and fill all those cracks in the walls and ceiling of the big bedroom. Then I coated the whole room with cream emulsion which had been lying in the store for longer than was good for it, applied two coats of matt white oil paint to the doors and windows and hung those elegant curtains. Regal, light and enormous it was, that room, and fit for a sultan. I introduced the carpet to the sea-wall where it nearly expired with its own dust under the beating, and me with it. Finally, I removed the smaller of the two beds and regaled the remaining big one with four blood-red blankets from the store. A teak table, wondrously carved and held up by two elephants, came from one of the smaller bedrooms and two rickety tables draped with another red blanket did service as a writing desk. In the store I found a genuine vintage Aladdin paraffin lamp with incandescent mantle intact. It was green with verdigris, missing a shade, and cracked in the chimney, but I rubbed it down with sand-paper, gave it two coats of the white oil paint and made a splendid cylindrical paper shade from a spare chart. It turned that room after dark into a veritable Aladdin's cave – a warm oasis of golden light with the big Jotul stove roaring away, stoked with driftwood logs gathered off the beach.

I tell you it was a palace. That first night alone, I lay listening to the island sounds that came filtering through, and me taking the measure of them. A steady north-westerly was drifting from Manish Strand, the sweep of sand up on the north shore, bringing the thunder of surf across the isle on the wings of the wind. It eddied round the old house, in the gutters, round the eaves, and through the tall ornate chimney-stacks. Somewhere below, a door gently banged.

I had brought a spare tilley lamp up to the room with me, still unlit, for I prefer the silent flame of a wick to the power-ful hiss of a pressure lamp. Lying there, picking out the sounds one from another, I was gradually aware of a new note in the increasing wind. Every now and then it would achieve a power great enough to skirl round something below my window with the resonance of an organ. I remembered that John, in talking of the island history, had mentioned a certain 'mad Captain' who delighted in parading up and down the sea-walk in front of the house with bagpipes at full blast. On Sundays too. This apparently so affronted the rest of the populace that dire forecasts were made as to the eventual resting place of his soul, for nobody is quite certain whether St Peter is a Scot.

As the power of the wind increased, so did the sound of that skirling come more and more to resemble the drone of the pipes, and it wasn't long before I had him in full Highland rig standing there outside my window, luring me out for a haunted hover over Borosdale with the long-since dead ghosts of the isle . . . and all the while that damned door banged . . . banged . . . somewhere below.

Now I'm not one for the haunts if you ask me quickly and in daylight, being of a mind that he who has a clear conscience is likely also to have a peaceful sleep at night. But this was all a bit much. Before long I was drawing those curtains back and peering out into the night, just to get the depth of my own idiocy. And still that benighted door banged. But now it became evident that the offensive thing was not in the house at all, but across the lawn in the barn . . . the barn in which John had surmised, with pregnant pause, that 'doubtless I'd be looking'.

I lit the tilley lamp and waited for it to go full blast and beaming, then put my dressing gown over a thick jersey and stuck my bare feet into seaboots. The stag's eyes followed me, twin points of light right down into the hall, as I clattered by on the bare wooden stairs. I took the keys from the kitchen, pushed the back door open against the wind – and stampeded three bullocks into the void. Across the back lawn a lovely stone archway – monastic in design – led from the garden to the greensward immediately below my warmly-lit bedroom window. The gate under the arch squeaked piercingly on its hinges as I pushed – and the bagpipes stopped dead! I don't mind you knowing it, I began to feel like a sack of cold wet tripe. What earthly normal phenomenon of wind playing about a guttering would stop its activity so abruptly at the warning sound of a creaking gate?

Shivering there in the bitter cold, centre of a pale oasis of dim light and kidding myself I wasn't frightened to death, there came into my mind a bit of doggerel I'd written when a child:

The pale weak beam of my lamplight flickers into the night, and by its glow I can only know those things which are close about – and even these are shadowy dim in the small unsteady light.
But out and beyond this circle, there is a world, I know. And it's none the less there because my lamp does not reach it with its glow.

Top, Lugworm with jury mizzenmast in 'house bay', Ensay, Outer Hebrides; *centre,* the homestead from behind the chapel on Ensay island, house bay on left; *bottom,* Taobh Deas, where the eagle had her eyrie. Photographed from Colla Sgeir reef

Above, left, one of the skeletons grinning up at me from the sands at Ensay; *right,* bringing *Obbe-Wobble* ashore. Low tide in house bay, Ensay; *bottom,* the peaks of Greaval and Roneval with Obbe in distance. From the top of Taobh Deas looking south-east

The light of my intellect flickers, into the blackness without.
And my reason is only a fitful flame which half shows a
truth, then it's lost again, in the endless darkness of doubt.
Yet little by little beyond the glow, Reality I find,
and it's none the less real because I fail to reach it with
my mind.

So again and again I try and try, to answer the timeless
question, Why?

Am I?

'You there!' I shouted into the windy void. 'Carry on
with your infernal dirge, and to hell with you!'
Silence.
A thousand points of light reflected from the glittering
mica faces in the rough-dressed stone of the old walls where
my own shadow danced and mocked me. A myriad daisy faces
peered at me, wan-white from the black grass. Insistently the
door of the barn continued its banging. I strode across, determined to persuade myself there was a rational explanation for
that sudden cessation of the pipes, but at the same time casting
a glance behind me to buttress my convictions. The barn door
was locked but loose on its fastenings and wobbling back and
forth. There was nothing handy to jam between the lintel and
the door, so I turned the key and pushed it back. Opposite
was a vertical ladder leading into a cavernous loft. A heap of
old clothing lay just inside the door and an indescribable as-
sembly of old junk was piled away to the left – rusty bedsteads, chains, rotting planks, a massive iron cooking range
and the mouldering remains of a mattress or two atop a cluster
of old packing cases. It was difficult to see in the lamplight
exactly what was heaped up there, but a crude wooden door
to my right evidently led into a division of the barn. Gently I
pushed it open.
At that moment a streak of white seemed to flash across
the top of the ladder. Instinctively I swung to face it and
backed through the door, peering up into the loft as I did
so.

Nothing. Nothing but the wind outside and the persistent hiss of my lamp. 'Imagination,' I said out loud to myself, and turned to examine the place. Then I stopped breathing. Honestly, you're not going to believe this but it's truth: ranged row above row on shelving from floor to ceiling were scores of grinning human skulls! On more racks in the centre of the room were piles of skeleton bones – tibias, fibulas, clavicles, humeri, ribs, pelvic saucers . . . clutch yourself – it was there, even down to the phalangea of the fingers and the ghastly eloquent mandibles, their teeth leering in silent laughter.

But what gave the whole nightmare a touch of the macabre was the fact that every skull, every pile of sifted bones, was enclosed in a transparent polythene bag neatly stapled at the top! It was hideous . . . Alfred Hitchcock hadn't got a look in, and *Psycho* seemed a health resort by comparison.

What would you have done?

I did. Cold, calm and calculated I edged out from that door, not daring to look back up that ladder for fear of seeing something too horrible to contemplate. I eased the door shut, locked it, and ran hell-for-leather back to the kitchen, slammed the door and locked it, grabbed a wood axe lying in the scullery and pushed back the passage door, ready for the worst. Slowly back along that mouldering corridor I crept, fearful that doors might swing open and reveal some frightful demented maniac with blood still clotted round his fetlocks, and I leapt up those stairs three at a time. The warmth and light of the room was like a haven. Slam went the door, and the sound of the massive key turning was the first reassurance since I left.

I lay back on the bed, trembling with cold – at least that's what I told myself and I'm sticking to it. 'There must be some logical explanation,' I muttered. John hadn't looked one bit like a depraved killer. My thoughts floated off to Dr Jeckyll and Mr Hyde. I switched on my portable tape recorder, but it was an unfortunate moment: Wagner's *Ride of the Valkyries* reverberated out. Hastily I changed the tape to Cleo Lane: I remember she was singing that hauntingly beautiful *I do miss you*.

I left the lamp on, turned low, lest it run out of paraffin

before dawn, for I'm sure nothing would have persuaded me from that room again till daylight...

Nothing, that is, except *Lugworm*. In my haste to get the place habitable I'd completely overlooked that she was due to float at high water – and her with but one anchor out at the top of the beach and the tides making! Hastily I looked at my tide-tables. High water was at three o'clock in the morning and I could hear the surge on the beach increasing in force as the level rose. The higher that tide rose, the greater would be those breakers on the beach: already it would be licking around her... if I disregarded it she would broach across the seas as they drove her up the beach... most possibly swamp her, not to dwell on the damage to her hull as she pounded. It was unthinkable.

Again I lit the Tilley lamp. There was an intermittent patter of rain now on the window and I remember wondering whether the cold raindrops would shatter the hot glass of the lamp. 'Dammit,' I thought, 'they must have got over that difficulty by now – but this is where I find out!'

The stag's head was positively laughing as I clattered down the stairs. This time I left by the porch door, and even the buffalo seemed to wear an amused grin. Outside it was bitter cold, wet, and the wind had risen even more. It was driving in across the Sound straight on to the beach. Casting a quick glance toward the barn, I nipped to the gate in the sea-wall and down the steps to the shore. *Lugworm* was just getting her chin wet with the top of the surge, and the breakers to the south of the bay sounded nasty. I swore at myself for not having laid out an anchor and dug it in well down the beach while the tide was low, for that way I could have waited till she floated, then pulled her easily off through the breakers into safe deep water. Mind you I'd still have had to swim ashore unless I stayed with her all the night. Now it looked as though I'd have to swim both ways, once to lay out the anchor seaward and once to get back ashore.

It's not the first time I've found myself in this situation on some beleaguered beach at unprintable hours dancing around like a watersprite. I put it down to experience, and have developed a technique for coping with the psychological side of the matter. I have to get angry. There was no other course left to me: the wind was onshore so I just HAD to move *Lugworm*'s anchor out there far beyond the breakers into deep water, return ashore and wait for her to lift with a swell, then heave her off quickly. The only alternative was to stay with her, keeping her bows into the breakers as she drove back up the beach on the rising tide. That would take hours. She was due to float within minutes.

I got angry. It helped to keep me warm in the rain, stripped and wading up to my earlobes with that anchor. Each successive surge floated the hair off the crown of my head! I dropped the anchor, pressed it in as far as possible with my foot. I remember as I swam back that the Tilley lamp was on the beach throwing a ghostly light on the rain and the white water along the strand. It picked out nothing more ... there was just me swimming in a black void, the glistening curtains of rain, the roar of the sea ahead and *Lugworm* silhouetted like a ghost ship ... beautiful beyond words, but pestiferously cold! Now *Lugworm* weighs all of a thousand pounds with the sailing gear aboard, and it's more than one chap can push. There was nothing more to do until she floated, so to keep warm I sprinted back and forth along the beach – three hundred paces one way and three hundred and fifty back – that's odd, I thought, has something gone rummy with space, too, on this incredible night? I think maybe it was my counting, but 'ere I'd checked it for certain *Lugworm* was swinging around in the surf. I leapt aboard and hauled taut on her anchor warp, waited for the next surge to come rolling in, and heaved. The anchor dragged home a foot or two, then held. She scraped a yard down the beach, then sagged deadweight again into the sand as the surge withdrew. The next one and the next failed to lift her. I was shivering now with cold, standing back on her stern deck to keep my weight aft, with the anchor warp through the bow fairlead to hold her stem into it. Down at the southern end of the bay I heard a real thumper come pounding in. 'Here it comes!' I told her. 'Lift this time, old girl, and we'll be afloat and away from danger.' And so it was.

I heard the thunder of that wave rolling northward round

the bay toward me, felt her tilt as the slam of white water hit her side, and suddenly the warp was slack in my hand. Heaving with all my strength, I brought fifty feet or more of it inboard. The Tilley lamp receded gently astern . . . our world grew quiet and we were alone in the deeps.

The warp grew taut again as it took her weight, and I waited to see how she would lie to the wind. The shore looked a long way off, but it couldn't have been much more than fifty feet: far enough to keep her afloat until the dawn As I swam back for a second time, strangely I was no longer in fear of ghosts, nor maniacs with hatchets: I could have met them all and laughed, and even played football with those pathetic skulls, for suddenly the world was an incredibly wonderful place, with every square inch of my skin tingling, and the blood pounding in my veins: so wide awake and glad to be alive was I . . .

I flicked the buffalo affectionately with my jersey, blew a kiss to the stag, and didn't even bother to lock my door before towelling down and burrowing into bed.

A brilliant beam is shafting straight overhead from the open window on to the cracked mirror above the fireplace. Reflecting off the water in the bay, it throws a shimmering net of light across the ceiling and walls. The whole room throbs with light.

In a mother-of-pearl sky the great luminous ball of sun is floating over the saddleback between Greaval and Roneval. A light north-west wind blows offshore, and there's *Lugworm* snoozing peacefully at full scope on her warp, streaming out into the bay and unlikely to take the bottom on this tide. The clock shows six-thirty: can it really be only three hours since the fiasco of last night?

Below the window a group of sheep are nibbling, attended by a frolic of lambs. Fourteen cows stand munching contentedly on the beach, still as statues. Aquatic cows. Contented aquatic cows, just peacefully being cows.

Through the south window I can see the green rise of the hill, and there's nothing but pale-blue sky above it. Unlimited sunlit space . . . unlimited freedom . . . and air like wine! I can see Dunvegan Head in Skye under a puff of cotton cloud twenty-five miles across the Minch – and the day is mine.

Scottish oatcakes, home-made butter and marmalade washed down with hot coffee does nothing to assuage one's appetite for life. The first thing, of course, was to investigate those skulls. In the brilliant daisy-fresh morning there was nothing macabre about them at all . . . it was quite clear they were relics from some burial ground, and so indeed it turned out: they had been recovered from the beach up on Manish Strand, where the encroaching sea had unearthed them, and were ready for reinternment when opportunity offered, hence the careful parcelling of bone with fellow bone, all meticulously marked – for what could be more frightful, I ask you, than being reburied with someone else's head?

I scaled the ladder into the loft, and there another spectre was nailed: no phantom was it I spied up there last night. The most worldly of wild white cats stared back at me from the recesses of a packing case, her yellow eyes glowing in the half-light. It was a mutual surprise, I would not have thought a cat could have survived alone on the isle – she never expected a visitation into the privacy of her sanctuary – yet totally alone she was, and doubtless her presence accounted for the absence of rats or mice or rabbits, for never a one did I see during my five months' stay! She was not keen to make my acquaintance, feeling doubtless somewhat trapped in her cell, so I retired, put a bowl of milk at the kitchen door and set off to investigate that other mystery: the origin of the bagpipes.

This was not so easy, for the wind had altered direction and was now but a light air, so the bellows were gone. But after a week or so I did find the cause, and it was fascinating. My assumption that the protesting squeal of that opening gate accounted for the cessation of the bagpipe was correct – though not in the fashion I imagined! the gate was made of tubular metal struts . . . need I say more? One end of a strut was open, and at a certain angle (when the gate was closed) this resonated like an organ pipe. By opening the gate I had simply altered its critical angle to the wind!

By ten a.m. the sun was hot enough to strip for a swim out to *Lugworm*. Something had to be done about her, for it was clear that she could not be allowed to take the ground in the seas which broke on that beach. I nearly ruptured myself helping two massive lumps of gneiss to roll down to a suitable spot beyond low water level. To these I secured a stout rope mooring, topped with a fisherman's orange float found in the rocks. With *Lugworm* tethered I felt a deal happier, knowing she would now take the bottom only at low water springs. At such state of tide all the surge would have gone from the sea anyway for it was then too shallow out in the narrows for much swell to penetrate.

There still remained, however, the problem of getting myself aboard the boat when the tide was in. That nocturnal swim had convinced me that 'enough is enough', for the water is mighty cold hereabouts. Somehow I had to construct a raft, or tender of sorts. There was a colossal log – the complete bole of a tree – up the beach by the sea-wall and it gave me ideas. But have you ever tried sitting athwart a smooth log when afloat? It might look fine on the cover of *Boy's Own*, but believe me, it doesn't work in practice, I tried it!

No, somehow I had to give birth to another *Ben* – and straightway set off to scour the beaches for suitable wood. An old dustsheet, eaten with moth, surrendered itself from the house and I knew from experience that this, when doubled, coated with oil paint and stretched over a framework of laths would make a fine light skiff. The laths were the problem. Search as I might, no pieces longer than three or four feet could I find among the piles of driftwood around the shores. There were, however, a few rotten planks from some ripped-out flooring in the barn, and though they must have been close on a century in age I reckoned with a bit of persuasion, when sawn into strips, I might get a vestige of 'turn' into them. It took me best part of two days, my fossicking about with a great driftwood fire under a ten-gallon pot of boiling water trying to get enough pliance back into them for a bend without snapping.

My antics did not go unnoticed. Clearly, the prolonged residence of one of the species homo sapiens was of more than casual interest to the true inhabitants of Ensay. The garden, with gates closed, was more or less stockproof, but my labours with the steaming-pot, that towering column of black smoke and my own exclamations of zeal, were carefully noted by some forty cows, Angus the bull, and all of the two hundred sheep not to mention uncountable lambs! They would stand, the cows, wide-eyed with their heads above the stone wall taking in every detail, sharing each triumph or defeat as plank after plank bent or snapped under my too-enthusiastic hands. The sheep clustered thick at the gates, and the lambs careless of mother's urgent warnings, would persist in gambolling through the bars in an effort to help! I tell you, it was better than a circus, both ways, and not for a moment were we any of us lonely. Indeed, so wondrous and filled with life was my new kingdom that it was difficult to tear myself away from her green sloping hillsides. Every clump of grass, every warm wind-sheltered hollow under a rock held a new miracle. I tell you, up here the sky is more than the sky: it's a blue immensity of sonic joy. Listen now and I can hear the distant whirring of the snipe as it plunges, its wings a-quiver, then lifts in an ecstasy of life high . . . high again up into the endless blue. There are redshank, greenshank, larks and rock-pippits. Hundreds – literally hundreds – of lapwings nesting in the low marshy field adjacent to the house. My movement across the isle is heralded by a flurry of wings and clamour of strident protest . . . and well it is so, for underfoot tiny red mouths gape up at me as I pass, expecting the worm which doesn't come, and one must tread warily to avoid tragedy in those minute homesteads.

But, despite these distractions, the skiff was eventually fashioned – there was about as much nature in those planks as in an Egyptian mummy – but with a load of hard swearing we got there in the end, and one memorable eve, just as day began flushing at the bold advances of night, why! *Obbe-Wobble* was born there on the beach, shaped like a laugh, painted sparkling white, eight feet in length and two feet six in the beam. Mighty fractious on the water she is, but fun . . . and the cows enjoyed her launching every bit as much as she and I!

It was about a fortnight later that I tore myself away and made a first sortie across to Obbe for provisions, bringing back a magnificent Highland beefsteak by way of celebration. I remember that steak well: better far than if I'd eaten it! Arrived once more at the isle, I stowed the groceries in the kitchen cupboard, but noticed a dust of white on the scullery floor. Close alongside was a bag of flour, pulled off the shelf, gnawed through and torn, and clear in the dust was the imprint of puss's feet! 'Little beggar,' I thought, 'but the poor thing must be ravenously hungry to tackle a bag of flour – lucky there wasn't anything else left about!' I put the steak on a plate and placed it in the window for coolth, then went to search for her. She was nowhere to be found. On return to the kitchen, a slight sound in the scullery alerted me – you get incredibly responsive to sounds when alone like this and (of course) there she was with the remains of my steak on the slate floor. She was in no doubt whatever that the steak belonged to me . . . that was obvious from her instant crouch of fear and surprise as I loomed up. But there was no way out of that scullery save the door, and I was athwart that. Gently I pushed it to behind me. We eyed one another.

'Puss!' I said, 'I've been waiting to be properly introduced, and now seems as good a time as any since you're evidently enjoying my hospitality regardless.' She didn't know what to make of it. Pangs of hunger drove her to the meat, pangs of fear drove her away from it. She was deplorably thin, looked hunted, and one ear was sadly torn from some ancient battle. I reckoned she was all of seven or eight years old. Very gently I moved to the shelf, took down an opened tin of milk, poured it into a cup, and added a little water from the tap, then placed it about three feet from her. She backed off, crouched against the wall, ready to claw my eyes out if need be. I picked up the gnawed remains of the steak, pulled it into small pieces, and passed them to her, one by one.

It was good to watch: seeing her adjusting to the unthink-

"OBBE-WOBBLE"

able . . . actually being given the very food she was so fur-
tively, fearfully, trying to bolt. We sat there in the scullery
together, neither of us missing a trick, until she'd finished
the meat and cautiously – always with one eye on me – emptied
the cup. Then I quietly opened the door and walked out.
Soon as I was far side of the kitchen she slunk through the
door, eased along the far wall, and bolted through the open
door. But I reckoned the battle was won!

For obvious reasons I christened her 'Grabbersnatch', and
kept a full bowl of milk at the ready outside the back door
with the odd titbit from the plate alongside. Soon my first
appearance each morning in the kitchen was greeted with a
wide-eyed little face peering through the leaded-light pane of
the door, and a truly deplorable attempt at a 'mew'. The poor
thing was so unused to any form of communication that her
vocal chords had jammed.

'You'll never make a Maria Callas,' I kept telling her, as
we got to know each other. It's astonishing how that cat put
on weight, cleaned herself up, adopted domestic habits and
conceded that there was much to be gained by trusting one
another. No sooner was she regularly fed than she gave up
the thieving, though I gave much thought to my wisdom in
this, for inevitably she would have to fend for herself again
one day. However, we solved this problem in another fashion,
of which you shall hear later. She was wonderful company,
and a rare and subtle form of communication came to operate
between us, for you don't need to verbalise to make yourself
understood: indeed, I'm convinced in some ways our much
vaunted articulation forms a positive barrier!

Within a week or two there was no corner of that isle, no
crevass in the rocky shore, nor slope of her green-topped
dunes that had not been explored. Up on the north shore, I
pondered the origin of that strange skeleton heap. Times gone,
it is said, the marauding Vikings came and had fine battles
hereabouts. But they were in a devil of a hurry, and had no
time to bury their dead. So one supposes the local populace
flung the corpses into a communal grave, and then the area
would gradually become a recognised burial place across the

years. Who knows when it all started? But the story goes that Viking artefacts have been found among the bones, and for sure I can vouch there to be a lot of bones under that sand yet, for was it not perhaps the skeletal shape of a marauding Norseman, I found gazing up at me from the sand one evening, as the sun went down? I found myself wondering just how many thousand times that sun had sunk obliquely below the horizon since those eyes had marvelled at it.

The weather was magnificent, and I went as bare as an aborigine, tanning to a deep mahogany, and becoming fitter with each day that passed, for there was always so much active physical work to be done. Fortunately, I had thought to bring with me a large bushman saw and an iron wedge, the latter for splitting the colossal logs which I sawed up and carried the mile back from Manish Strand. So gradually a haystack of driftwood piled up in the garden, each bit of a size to slip into the bedroom stove. The evenings were a balm. Only one real meal was necessary in the day, and I took this when the sun had gone down, then lit the lamp upstairs and got down to the writing. After a bit Grabbers discovered the warmth of the room, too, and would hesitantly creep up and curl beneath the feet of the stove, but always I left the doors ajar so that she could get out during the night, for her hunting instincts

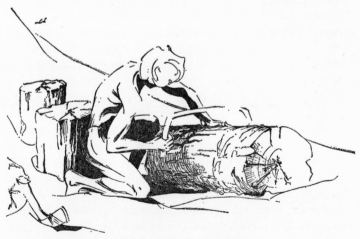

. . . so much active physical work to be done

103

remained very strong. Frequently she would awaken me in the early hours of the morning with a positive crow of pride as she brought a wildly flapping chick bird up to the room for me to share! I would take it gently from her mouth, for she was not really hungry and, in fact, seldom hurt the bird; often it would fly off through the window, the wiser no doubt for the event.

So the weeks passed, and the multitude of eggs in the nests hatched. I followed their development with the camera, taking hundreds of colour slides, getting to know the chicks, sharing in their adventures as they grew. There was one large nest of seaweed bottomed with sheep's wool in a cliff on the north-west corner of the isle, and four blue-and-brown speckled eggs hatched into the ugliest little bare-pink chicks the day after I found it. Always, long before I had stalked or sprinted across the maidan of grass, the lapwings and the oystercatchers had warned the parent birds of my approach – and no sign did I ever see of them while the chicks were growing up. It was fascinating to watch the development of those skinny little forms. Within two days the faintest puffs of white fluff appeared, slowly the pink skins turned grey, then metallic blue. They looked for all the world like primaeval pterodactyls in miniature, so leathery did they become with their stringy necks and ever-gaping blood-red mouths. Two weeks after discovering them I took the most developed from the nest and photographed him on the grass; he didn't object in the least, though I christened him Grumpy, for reasons which you'll see. Three weeks later, while peeling a turnip in the house, I heard an unusual conversation taking place out in the garden. It was hoarse, guttural and astonishingly articulate, but quite unlike any voice I'd yet heard on the isle. On top of the garden wall were two of the biggest hooded crows I've ever set eyes on. They were sizing up the place, and my presence at the door spurred them to yet more articulation. Together they eyed me up and down, with obvious interest, croaking to one another as they did so. Satisfied, they took off and flew back to the north shore, and the mystery was solved.

Fraser Darling, in his book on the wild life of the Hebrides, states that this *corvus cornix* is one bird we can do without, and I'm not arguing. Nevertheless, I had become very fond

104

of Grumpy and his brood and could no more have wrung their necks than my own. A month to the day after hatching they took to the wing, and that was the last I ever saw of them.

The days floated by, each one a more wonderful experience than the last. Each brought its own problems, its own demands, and whatever else was in hand there was always the continuing search for driftwood fuel. But the peace of the place is beyond description. I gathered a sackful of sheep's wool off the grass slopes, washed it and filled two pillowcases – I'm sleeping on them yet – and made a splendid six-foot lance from a bamboo cane found on the beach, tipped with the wing-feathers of an enormous gannet found dead on Manish Strand. It was splendid skill and exercise, slinging that lance from the top of the dunes down to a target drawn in the sand below.

Come evening, I'd spend hours lying on the warm faces of those dunes, just watching miracles of colour as the sun went down, for by now all the hysteria, all the compulsive drive to be 'doing', had fallen away from me.

'Doing' there was, and enough – seldom in my life have I physically worked harder than those months alone on the isle – but the days were a rhythm of rewarding practical effort, while the evenings were a rhythm of ease. Night time, I wrote. It's amazing how little sleep one requires when you're really fit, totally involved with your environs, and alone. Gregariousness takes its toll of us: we pay for the masks we adopt, the parts we play in social and business intercourse.

I spruced up the old house, giving all the windows and doors a scrape down, then three coats of white paint. She began to smile again. The sea-wall, breached at the northern end, was rebuilt and all the garden gates were rehung and painted. The kitchen – dark, dirty and forlorn – didn't know what hit it! Bucket after bucket of springwater sluiced over the walls, draining countless years of grime away, and a coat of whitewash followed by two coats of white emulsion paint did wonders. It fairly glowed with the evening sun coming through the newly painted window. Bathing was a problem. The Rayburn was splendid – but used a colossal amount of wood, and coal was both prohibitively expensive and difficult to get across

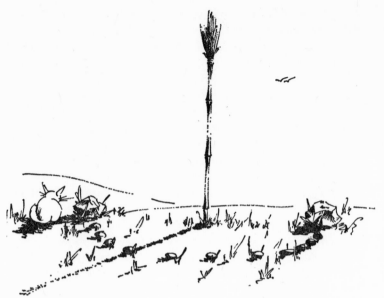

What need of a clock when one has a splendid sundial?

to the isle, so I would boil up the ten-gallon iron pot on a driftwood fire and tip it into a four-foot diameter galvanized bathtub found in the storeroom. There, on the lawn – watched always by the cows – I would splash to my heart's content . . . and to the delight of Grabbersnatch, who viewed the whole matter with incredulity.

A month slipped by, but time itself stood still. Indeed, it was a week before I discovered my clock had stopped. But what need of a clock when one has a splendid sundial on the lawn made from the bamboo lance and a circle of beach pebbles to tell all that was necessary: one rock for breakfast and the 0630 shipping forecast, a second for the evening forecast and a third for my own supper and a bowlful for Grabbersnatch . . . that slim shadow, shortening gradually as spring turned to ripe summer, told me all I needed to know.

My radio, remembered haphazardly at news time, occasionally re-introduced an alien outside world . . . bomb mutilation in a metropolis, violence at some mass hysterical sporting event . . . political bickering, strikes, greed for more and more possessions. It was like tuning in to some sick horror play, and I found it hard to believe this was the real world of men, from which, for a moment, I had managed to escape.

The marsh dried up, the fields grew mellow, and many of the chicks were flown. The lambs grew fat and the calves were young bullocks. Angus grew a bit thinner, worn out doubtless by a harem of forty to one, and still the weather held.

Eventually an unwelcome missive arrived from the world of business, calling me away for a week to Oban, and it was now that I realised the gulf between this real life on the isle to which I had become accustomed and that urgent artificial strife back in the world of Man. Such a headlong plunge once more into the hysteria of 'civilisation', with the ferries, the buses, the trains, the snatching of synthetic meals between connections, fish-and-chips in packed noisy cafés, and the horrific queueing for tickets, jostling for sitting space, rushing ever rushing . . . all that is accepted as part of living in overcrowded communities suddenly had become unbearable to me. You may imagine I was glad to return to my kingdom, where life still had some dignity.

In fact, that return to the isle led to an experience I'll not forget. Having thankfully arrived by ferry at the southern tip of South Uist, I set off walking northward on a Sunday with the intention of making the shore of the Sound sometime on Monday from where a small ferry connects with Harris. It was a long walk – some forty miles if I remember rightly – and would not have been accomplished by the time of the Monday ferry but for two very acceptable lifts on the lonely road. The day was mild but grey, with a swirling mist driving in from sea which made the incredibly barren landscape even more desolate and lonely than is usual. However, I had properly got into the swing of the walking and had already crossed the stone causeway that joins South Uist to Benbecula. The road was a single-track affair with passing places every quarter of a mile or so, and there was nothing to be seen but the dark ribbon ahead and the grey rocky hillside sloping up from the sea. What then appeared at first sight to be a tall cypress tree in the mist to my right aroused some curiosity. As I drew closer it turned out to be a truly colossal statue – some forty feet high, standing quite alone on the rock, with no plaque nor inscription, rail or plinth. It was the Virgin and Child, and of course I had to leave the road to take a closer look, so unexpected was it to find such a thing on this barren little isle. It was made from blocks of what seemed to be granite, but what was so remarkable was the face of the Virgin. I have seen the structure thereof in a thousand 'hippie' girls far and wide, for it was essentially a twentieth-century maid ... but never before have I seen what shone from there. In that girl's face was all the strength and pride of absolute purity. She looked over my head as I craned backward to catch the miracle ... over my head ... and out to sea.

Standing in the crook of her right arm, with his left hand resting on her shoulder, was the Christ child. A babe? No: far more than that. A young boy? Hardly – yet. But I tell you, I couldn't stop looking at that face! In the mist it glistened, almost glowed, high up there on the girl's shoulder ... and somehow the sculptor had captured an infinite power and authority therein.

One does not expect to see this in the granite face of a young child. One may ask how any mortal can capture infinity in anything, let alone in a granite rock. But, of course, the miracle lies not in what the chisel had put *into* the features – but what, in his wisdom, the sculptor had left *out*. Something far greater than the hand of man had infused into that half-sketched face not just a sense of mystery, though that would have been wonder enough, but a shining omniscience ... a depth of *understanding* that lifted the heart, with hope.

As I looked at Him, I understood – so far as any human being may be said to 'understand' the real meaning of love. The real power and the glory of it. Through that face came the joy of everything to which we *ought* to aspire, and to which we seldom give even a chance thought.

The Virgin was slim and robed down to the ground, so that the eye filled in the exquisite stance as she took the weight of the child. The child was holding up one hand in blessing. Blessing us.

So I walked back down toward the rocket missile test range that lies between the girl's feet and the shore of that lovely isle, and caught the ferry back to Ensay.

Top left, bathtime on the lawn, Ensay, watched by Buttercup; *right,* 'Grumpy'; *centre,* Ensay isle from Taobh Deas, looking southward. Killegray and North Uist in right background; *bottom,* great boles of trees to be sawn and carried a mile from Manish Strand to the house. Pabbay isle in distance

Top, the hills of North Uist looking south-west from Manish Strand; *centre,* piping the betrothed from the chapel to the house, Ensay isle

bottom, 'Grabbersnatch', the true Laird of Ensay

Chapter Five

The Sound of Harris

It was good to get back to my isle. The name *Ensay*, in Norse, means Isle of Meadows, and how appropriately those ancient Scandinavians placed their labels. The ending *ay* is Norse for island, but it's said that the name of the whole group – the Hebrides – is Roman in origin and brought to its modern spelling by a printer's blunder: The original Roman name was *Hebudae*, or *Ibudae*. The 'I' (pronounced 'E') signified an island, while the *budae* was quite possibly derived from the Celtic word *muid*, meaning sea-spray, or misty foam, which is surely appropriate enough. The Roman writers mention these isles under the name *Hebudes* and the story goes that the 'u' became accidentally printed 'ri' which would certainly account for the current name.

Misty isles they are at times, but oh! when Phoebus smiles his light has a clarity and astringent quality akin to Swiss mountain sunlight. The early Celts showed remarkable perception when they referred to this far-flung string of jewels as *Tir-an-og*: the 'Land of Youth'. It burns deep that sun, and rich, seeming to reverse the very process of ageing, helped by the clear air and silence. Then it draws a blanket of mist to protect the freshness from too harsh a parching.

I have found that people think of the isles as being excessively wet, but in fact the rainfall up here in Scotland is now only an average of thirty-five inches per year, which is some ten inches less than it was in the 1940s – and well below the average rainfall for Cornwall. One wonders what degree of coastal erosion is taking place on the prevailing weather side of the isles; certainly the rate here on Manish Strand is appalling. But wherever sand forms the margin of the land

E   109

there must inevitably be a rapid shifting and doubtless deple-
tion at one point (as at the burial ground) is often offset by
accumulation at another. But the erosion by the seas of rock
itself is a one-way process. Old gneiss, of which the majority
of these isles and hills is formed, is a very hard laminated
rock of quartz, feldspar and mica; some of the oldest rock on
the Continent. Even so, the inexorable process of erosion
continues. Often as I sit watching the assault at high water on
this sea-wall below my bedroom window, I wonder how any
man-made structure can withstand such force. A hundred and
thirty years ago, on the Atlantic rock of Skerryvore before the
lighthouse was begun, a systematic measurement of the pounding of the waves was made. The average summer weight of
pounding was 611 lb. per square foot, while the winter
average was 2,086 lb. per square foot. In a south-
westerly gale in March 1845 it reached 6,083 lb. per square
foot!

The tidal flow of water hereabouts is interesting too. Generally speaking, through this Sound of Harris in summer the
stream at neaps flows from the Atlantic during the whole
of the day, and from the Minch during the night. In winter
the process is largely reversed. Spring tides, however, both
summer and winter, tend to flow from the Atlantic for the
greater part of the time that the tide is rising (but never for
more than five and a quarter hours) and then flows back into
the Atlantic during most of the fall of the tide. Between the
isles in constricted water, such as the caolas skaari channel just
south of Ensay, the velocity reaches up to five knots at springs
and not much less at neaps. In the broader channels it runs
around two or two-and-a-half knots. Navigation hereabouts
has to be an exact science, most especially in slow-moving
craft, and deep-keelers are a nightmare. There must be no
Dead Reckoning: constant runs on available transits, and
continual fixing is the order of the day if one is not completely
familiar with the topography of the rocks. It's madness to
approach the Sound in poor visibility.

In Leverhulme's time, due to his ambition to turn Obbe into
a major commercial fishing port, it's said that it was easier
to navigate through the Sound at night than it was in daytime.
The lighthouses he had built on the isles are, however, no

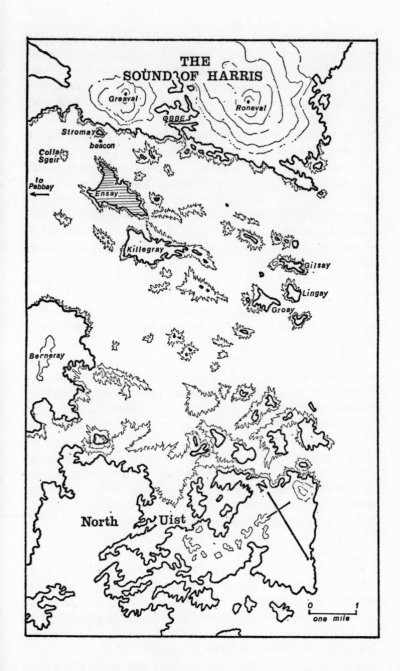

THE
SOUND OF HARRIS

Greaval

OBBE

Roneval

Stromay
beacon

Colla
Sgeir

to
Pabbay

Ensay

Killegray

Gilsay

Lingay

Groay

Berneray

North   Uist

N

0   1
one mile

longer lit, but they do give convenient bearings for a mariner in daytime.

But apart from the running stream, *Lugworm* could laugh at the rest of these hazards, for as I've said, her draught is less than a yard at her most profound, and under a foot when she's shallow.

She has confidence now, for we have had time enough to take soundings in this area of the 'misty isles', and already my crisp new chart is a battered, limp and salty sheet, barely legible, or for that matter necessary, for there is no kelp-ridden reef, nor knife-edged rock, nor lonely islet with its mantle of grass and boggle-eyed ewe that has not been prodded, examined, landed upon and generally assessed in relation to these awesome tides, sluicing like some oceanic millrace through the isles.

You would be void of imagination too if, when the mists come swirling in from the Atlantic, you didn't find your eye lifting for the ghosts of those long lean Viking ships nosing in with the flood to plunder and rape and make merry hell at high water by carrying off the local girls. Damned fine prizes those girls must have made, too, if the samples I've seen on my travels are anything to judge by, for they have a liveliness about them, bright eyes and a bold, lithe manner of carrying themselves that turn a man's head despite himself.

Speaking of hazards, have you ever sniffed the ozone down to leeward of a Hebridean reef at low-water springs, when the mists come creeping in so heavy and silent over a mirror-sea that you just sit for hours listening ... until the roar of over-falls from the running tide two miles away brings you to your senses? Ah, but it's an evocative, dank scent that sets just the right tone for that flesh-creeping dirge that comes floating from the rocks beyond the border of your visible world ... rising, like the hair on the nape of your neck, as it gains volume by another and another great cow seal joining the unearthly lament. Eerie and echoing the ululation comes, like wails from the bottom of the Pit. I tell you, if it were to this that Jason was listening when he had to lash himself to the mast then he must have been pretty desperate, poor chap, for it's enough to curdle you before breakfast!

But this morning there are no mists, nor wailing, for there

112

is *Lugworm* in the bay, with the sun flinging a brilliant new day straight over the ridge of Roneval out there on Harris, and rippling down the Sound comes the first kiss of a brisk north-easter that sets the burgee at her gaff chattering and exhorting me to choke on the oatcakes and scatter crumbs and marma-lade, so eager is she to cast off the mooring and wing away to the north and west. For has Pabbay Isle not beckoned too long, unanswered?

So she spread a glad genoa, main and mizzen, took *Obbe-Wobble* in tow and together we beat out from the bay over toward Greaval, not putting in the final tack till the barnacles on Stromay were flinching and the water frowning black under the cliffs . . . and then we were out northward between the beacon reef and the islet with the spring ebb giving us a useful thrust through the overfalls.

Out to the broad mouth of the Narrows we reached, where Colla Sgeir reef lifted a curling white hand in salutation. It broke creaming close aboard as we ran westward and there were thundering breakers on Manish Strand where the beach was a steaming stretch of white in the morning sun, backed by bastions of green-topped dunes.

Oh Neptune! It was one of those mornings when you catch the world laughing with her hair down; bright, clear blue above, deep, rolling turquoise below, and all about was the green and gold brilliance of the isles. I tell you the sky sang a song in our sails that day, with *Obbe-Wobble* leaping and dancing astern, agog at the wonder of such a mighty ocean.

We had in mind to make a landing close behind the reef at Rubh'a'Bhaile Fo Thuath on Pabbay's eastern point, but not one of the three of us could quite get our tongue round it, so we made a bit of southing until Shillay hid behind Pabbay to warn us (as if we didn't know) that we were approaching the shallow sandbar that joins that isle and Berneray. But the ebb was hand-in-hand with the wind so the seas only heaped up a bit, and *Lugworm* cocked up her stern and surfed down the face of them with a quick glance now and then to the tiddler astern who rode the waves like a gull. Before you could cry 'Tir-an-Og' we were off the tongue of Rubh'an t-Seana-chaisteil rocks and nosing into their lee. Down plunged the anchor through two fathoms of crystal green – and up

113

shot an astonished dab to streak off and warn his brothers of this rare intruder.

After all that boisterous wet splother of wind and open water our world was suddenly still, and warm, and silent. The heat from that beach was so inviting it demanded an instant casting off of the last bits of clothing before I pulled ashore to sprint along the hot sands while the salt chalk-dried on my skin and there came that rare and carefree sense of well-being only those susceptible to a strange island madness can know.

Pabbay is uninhabited. Have you, I wonder, ever landed like some explorer of old on the sleeping beaches of an uninhabited isle? There were two miles of them to be combed and armfuls of silvered driftwood to be loaded for the house fires. There were strange bottles, too, of all shapes and colours, misted by years of rolling in the sand, any of which MIGHT have contained messages, but none of which did, and fishermen's floats of all conceivable patterns. A dinosaur might have filled her jewellery chest from the magic of that beach ... and probably did, times gone.

In the heat of early afternoon I was casting an eye on the inviting green rise of the isle and I set off through the bee-buzzing grass and heather, up past the first gaunt shoulders of grey gneiss and still on up to where, from a sheltered hollow, there erupted an explosion of wild stags, or hind, or I'm damned if I know exactly what they were, so shattered was I at the shower of grit from the thudding hooves of those powerful antlered beasts. Only the fact that they were in full flight enabled me to pluck up courage and stagger on up to that final shoulder from which I could see the rounded tip of the island. Then, breathless and gulping in glittering air, there was nothing more above, but the whole world laid out below right round the full sweep of the horizon. Such a view you have not seen, nor ever will see, save you have the luck ever to stand on the tip of Pabbay on a golden summer day. What pale ghosts are these photos!

Northward, Shillay voyaged majestically through the ocean, her wake of white froth streaming astern on the now strong north-east running flood. Her emerald green top rose in a long slope, breaking off sharp at the western edge to plummet in vertical cliffs down to and beneath the turbulent water.

114

I could see the dots of white sheep grazing on her slopes, for every isle with a cargo of grass must sustain its moneyspinning crew of breeding ewes and a ram or two. Southward lay mile upon mile of empty beach on Berneray, with the unbelievable blue of Lochs Bruist and Borve shimmering behind acres of machair. As a backcloth to that, rolling down to the horizon and far beyond was the full panoply of the Uists and Barra, with Mount Marrival and Eaval crouched like sentinels either side of towering Hecla, monarch of them all, thirty miles off.

The brilliance of that southern aspect made me turn my eyes away from the sun, and it was then I caught far out – like a distant lonely ghost haunting the horizon – the mist-blue peaks of St Kilda. Even at that distance, some fifty miles off, I could sense the grandeur of those cliffs. Dishabited this forty years and more, so strong is the call still from this most remote of the Outer Isles that a band of volunteers, so I'm told, go annually to maintain and take a spark of summer life back to its deserted village.

So I sat bewitched by the immensity and freedom of it all until the western flanks of Lewis and Taransay away to the north-east began to take flame in the evening light; and there far below lay *Lugworm* – a tiny black thing with faded red mizzen – key to so many adventures in far-off places over the years . . . but not any one of them, I truly believe, more worthwhile or beautiful than this.

It was late before we could tear ourselves away from that isle. As we ghosted quietly off the beach my eye, searching the dark outline of the hill, caught the motionless silhouettes of the deer, still as statues watching our going, and wondering . . . timid but overpoweringly curious as to the nature of these strange visitors.

The sun was a red ball above the amber misty horizon as we re-crossed the bar and made our easting with a dying wind. Clouds, rolling slowly in from sea, awoke with shock on the weather flanks of Taransay. There they took fire, leaping into the vault of sky in crimson flames as though to toast the toes of the Gods themselves. And the sea went quiet, and the islands held their breath in silent awe at the majesty of it.

We plucked a fine 'cuddie' – which you or I might wrongly

call a pollack – from the dark kelp three fathoms down in Caolas Skaari channel west of Ensay. Then the sails had to drop, for the ebb tide was winning and the outboard tipped us round the southern end of the isle until we could nose back quietly under sail with the help of the stream to House Bay.

So it was poached fillet of cuddie in white sauce, washed down with a pint of Rodel beer beside a crackling driftwood fire – and Grabbersnatch appreciating the head and tail every bit as much as I did the middle. That night the yellow beam of my oil lamp probed from the window of this cavernous old mansion until the early hours of the morning with only the inquisitive seals out there with *Lugworm* wide-eyed in wonder at the rat-a-tat of this typewriter.

'Grabbers,' I mused, one rainy noon in early July, 'our monk-like solitude is about to be infringed!' She stopped playing the harp on the middle of my bed and looked at me in disbelief. 'I'm not at all sure, my little whitened sepulchre, that you'll be sleeping on that bed much longer at that!' I added.

B. was due to arrive at Obbe. It was about time, too, for solitude is absolutely splendid, but a bit tedious when you have to suffer it alone for long periods.

'Sharing takes the sting out of life,' I philosophised, while Grabbersnatch recommenced her ablutions. 'Fact is, there are limits to what a man should suffer in the cause of literature . . . you're all right, all you do is eat and you evidently find the island life completely to your taste. I'm different.'

With Grabbers you never quite know exactly what line her philosophy takes. Expressive she is, in everyday mundanities, but she retains a womanlike subtlety when it comes actually to committing herself in matters of the heart. She has, in fact, developed an appalling purr and an endearing habit of rubbing her head affectionately against my hand as I fill up her bowl of milk. And then, as last night, she will drain my soul of love by snatching the sausages actually out of the pan on the stove, an act of sheer rebellion if ever I saw one, for hungry she is NOT.

'If you take my tip, you'll cultivate B. with every catlike

ploy you can bring to bear, otherwise you're due for a change in your standard of living.' She stalked out, tail erect. If ever an animal said, 'Who's here on sufferance, anyway?' she did at that moment.

So there was B., rucksack at the hoist, waving from the end of the quay in Obbe, for the bus was early, and *Lugworm* rammed the quay in exuberance of the moment.

'What's the fishing like?' she queried, as we corkscrewed off Soundwards. 'Have you missed me?' I ask you?!

'I'm a piscatorial pundit,' I boasted. 'You name it – there's cod, mackerel, skate, ray, dogfish, ling, tunny, haddock, coalfish, hake, halibut and herring ... not to mention saithe and lythe ... and I bet you don't know the difference?'

'They're both a form of pollack, only the saithe has a straight line down its side and is good eating, while the lythe has a wiggly line and tastes like cotton wool.' I was flabbergasted. 'Been reading it up,' she laughed, 'and so, evidently, have you. So you've been living on fish?'

'Two: a fine fat salmon that jumped into the boat and brained itself and a cuddie, which is a young coalfish – and I don't know which I enjoyed most. Meet Grabbers.'

There she was, sitting at the tideline, demure and obviously whisker-deep in domesticity, exhuding a positive halo of good manners.

'Ah! *Fucus vesiculosus*,' shouts B., leaping ashore and clutching a mangy bit of weed. 'Bladderwrack to you ... used in the lazy beds.' She's quite nutty about seaweed and even eats some of it. 'And look here: *pelvestia canaliculata*. The cows will be down on these beaches, they love it.' I stared at her in sheer admiration. Grabbers stalked off in high dudgeon.

And so it went on. I learned more in a few days about the birdlife and weed on that isle than I'd assimilated all summer. B. devours information like a snowplough and distributes it in much the same fashion. 'You've got to take an intelligent interest in your surroundings,' she's constantly telling me. 'It's no good just looking at things and dreaming about them. Man didn't evolve on philosophy – he used his teeth.'

'Very well,' I ruminated, a day or two later. 'If it's participation you're after, there's a clutch of cormorants' nests down on Gilsay isle that might still have young, or even eggs in them. They're inaccessible to normal man . . . hidden under a stinking guana-covered cliff. We'll sail down there with the camera; I need a photo for one of the books.

So it came about that four days after she arrived we packed a bottle of wine and oatcakes in *Buggerlugs* and set off southward down the Sound. Killegray cost us an hour, frolicking on the beaches for shells, and a lazy liquid lunch in a grotto on the west shore of Lingay put us to sleep for a couple more, but after things were straight again we could see, across the mirrorlike water, that the southern cliffs of Gilsay were vibrant with activity. Some forty or fifty cormorants were engaged in urgent traffic 'twixt cliffs and sea. We could make out the whitened slopes below the nests, which were tucked under an overhanging brow. Even from that distance it looked a bit of a challenge.

'How do you propose getting near enough to take a photo?' B. asked. 'You've no telephoto lens and it's impossible to climb down there from above – you'll break something. Is it worth it?'

'What are we here for?' I countered. 'We've not come to the Arctic Circle just to look at things and dream about them. I'll use my teeth!'

Hah! Prophecy and teeth must be two of my strong points. It was plain on arrival that the nests were indeed inaccessible from above. We stooged about in *Lugworm* with *Obbe-Wobble* in tow examining the cliff face. There was just one possible access down a fissure on to some great bluffs to one side of the cliff foot. After that I might climb up an excreta-covered slope on to a narrow ledge which ran below the overhanging brow and passed just under the nests. Protesting adults launched their ungainly forms out, dropping to within feet of the water before becoming properly airborne, and the place was resonant with cries echoing off those black rock faces – every bit as good as the Albert Hall.

'There's nothing else for it,' I enlightened B. 'Far too risky to take *Lugworm* against those rocks. We'll have to anchor off the shingle beach backalong and I'll go ashore. Then you row *Obbe-Wobble* back here beneath the nests and be ready to pick up the bits if need be, for if disaster strikes I'll be swimming after a bounce or two.' I could see she was unhappy. To start with, she hadn't really got used to *Obbe-Wobble* (nor *Obbe-Wobble* to her) so that in itself would be quite an adventure. She demurred.

'It isn't me I'm thinking about,' I remonstrated. 'It's the blessed camera. Do you think the insurance company will cough up for a total loss claim when they hear it's been dangled over the weather side of the Hebrides? My bet is it'll be an 'act of God' somewhere in the small print. No: you station yourself just below the nests and I'll try not to land in the skiff when I fall. I'll fling you the camera as I pass, but for heaven's sake keep it dry.'

It was the work of minutes to gain the greensward above the cliffs, but the descent down that narrow fissure was a bit hungry on the skin. I knew it would be impossible to re-ascend by the same means, but counted on being able to hand the camera to B. in the skiff, having taken the photos, and then swimming back to *Lugworm*. It was cold under those cliffs and the long swell that rolled in kept licking over the slimy rocks which had to be traversed before I could tackle the slope up to the ledge. It's not easy leaping over wet weed-covered rocks at the best of times, but with a very expensive camera dangling round your neck it's quite lethal, for it upsets the balance. Meanwhile, B. was carving an erratic course from *Lugworm* in my general direction, helped by my exhortations. By the time she finally drifted under the nests I was impatient to start climbing.

'Stay exactly where you are, darling – just be ready to grab the camera if things go wrong,' I counselled. The place reeked of dead fish. Acrid and pungent, it was, and before long I was plastered with the white porridge that lay thickabout. But the nests were there just above me and there were cracks on that slope that you could get a toe in here and a finger there. Provided they stayed that way I saw no reason why I should not work up to, and then along, the ledge. I got up to its level, and all that remained was to ease round a knuckle of rock close under the overhanging roof, then inch farther along to the actual nests. I could see nothing to stop me. But then, as I remember, from where I was I couldn't quite see right round that knuckle either.

Halfway round, poised above the dark water far beneath, I began to have sickening doubts. You know the feeling? Every thought in your head focuses on the worst of all possible events. I saw myself bouncing off rock faces, mangled to a pulp and the camera ruined ... B. with a measly widow's pension and a photo on the piano ... all that sort of thing. One twinge of cramp in a brace of toes and it would be stark fact! My legs and arms went limp, the bones jellified as I clutched the rock and sweated. Could I get back? Could I get forward? The question was academic, for certain I couldn't stay spreadeagled on that knuckle for more than seconds ... either was better than the present predicament. Below me, B. was fossicking about in circles trying to stay within range. I was in a smelly mess. To be brave in retrospect, I think it was the camera that really worried me: you don't lightly fling yourself into space clutching six months' hard earnings. I began breathing deeply to calm myself. 'B.,' I called after a while, trying to make my voice sound casual. 'Do you think you can get vertically beneath me and catch the camera if I drop it?'

'But what about YOU?' she gasped. She had a point. One hiccup and there would be me, her, *Obbe-Wobble* and the camera all fulminating with the bubbles. 'Can't you slide on to that ledge just to your right ... It looks easy from here!' she called.

That did it. Suddenly I knew I wasn't going to drop anything, much less me. There was nothing more to be lost than absolutely everything, and I was more likely to lose that by staying where I was than by going on. Sheer logic inched me round the knuckle 'till I lay gasping on the safety of that ledge. Ahead, the cormorants were in pandemonium. Leathery chicks slithered from the nests, scrabbling to hide themselves in dark crevasses. One nest, close under the roof, still held three porcelain-like eggs. It was a study in white, sepia and glistening rock. I worked carefully along, full-length on the slimy ledge and adjusted the meter reading. The light was magnificent: the viewfinder captured all the wild desolation, the sheer inaccessibility of that place. Hard and sharp I focused on the eggs from about two feet off. A

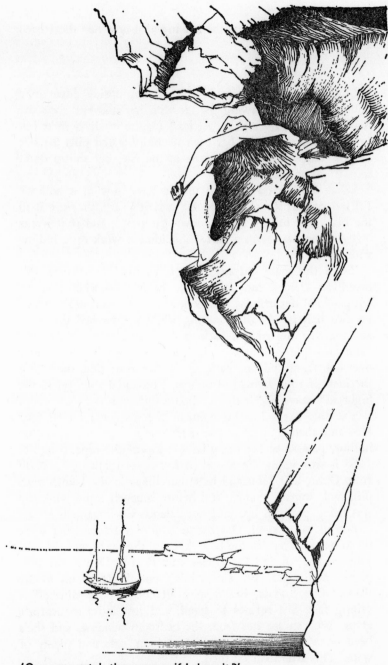

'Can you catch the camera if I drop it?'

winner, that photo. You'd be looking at it now had there been a film in the camera.

Bluebell has the staggers. I found her upside down in a hollow last week, pawing the air with her hooves: she's the russet cow with liver fluke. At least I think it's liver fluke but I'm no farmer . . . John has been feeding her red pills the size of golf balls this last two visits to the isle, but things don't seem to get any better.

What do you do with an upside-down cow in a hollow? I'll tell you what: you parbuckle her. It's easy, they use it in the Navy for rolling barrels down gangways, and if it works down a gangway with a barrel shouldn't it work up a hollow with a cow?

'Fetch the spare halyard from *Lugworm*,' I instructed B., breathless from a run half across the isle. 'Bluebell's in the out-patients' department and bellowing her head off!' I made up two halters of rolled sacking while she fetched the rope, and together we trudged back to the source of the bellowing. 'The principle is simple,' I instructed B. 'We'll put a halter over one front and one back leg on her same side, then fling the loop of rope across her tummy. You and I then get in the bight and heave like hell. She should roll over.'

She did. For a blissful moment she staggered on all four feet and then . . . you've guessed? She rolled back into that hollow, pawing at the seagulls! On top of the rope.

So it was across the Sound in *Lugworm* for a rescue party from Obbe, and John and half the village in the launch with pills and stomach pumps, and before Bluebell could wink she was being propped up until her balance was regained.

But all to no avail. Day before yesterday I found her stuck up to her kneecaps in the bog. 'She has the death wish,' I told John, and again half the village embarked in Don's boat with planks and ropes. We sledged her out this time on to the flanks of Borosdale, but despite all efforts poor Bluebell is failing fast. She refuses to stand, and just looks mournfully at us. We can see her from the bedroom window, and she's been on a vitamin-enriched diet of bran, oats and plenty of water. This afternoon she died.

'It happens,' I consoled B. 'Better to go fast like that than slide downhill slowly!' But what do you do with a dead cow on Borosdale?

A boatload from Obbe dragged the corpse to the shore, and then sixty rampaging horses in Don's launch towed her out to the broad Atlantic for a sea funeral with full ceremony, and that was that.

This morning up the hill there was a fat ewe on her back. 'We got here in time,' I told B. as we rolled her over and held her steady 'till she got her bearings again. 'If they can't get up they soon exhaust themselves trying, and then down come the blackback gulls and peck out their eyes . . .' 'Stop!' she exclaimed, 'I don't want to know.'

'But it's nature, and no good our putting on blinkers,' I remonstrated. 'Just because homo sapiens keeps reality at arm's length doesn't change it, and it's going on all the time. On this earth one thing lives by the death of another, and that's the order of things: we can't change it. If creatures are to evolve, then it must be by survival of the fittest. If they don't evolve they cease to be. That's the choice.'

'Then it were better not to be,' she answered.

I thought about that. There must be something wrong with our morality, or else God's got it all mixed up. But B. and I have had this discussion before and there's no answer to it. Maybe we're just asking the wrong questions . . . so off we went to sunbathe up on Manish Strand and saw up a few more logs, and there was glory in it all, and to hell with philosophy.

Chapter Six

The Wedding

Now I must tell you that within a hundred yards of the old house there is a little chapel standing on the greensward looking across the Sound. There has been a chapel here, so they tell me, since 800 A.D. and dedicated to St Columba. For many years it was a stable, but recently has been refurbished by my friend the Doctor, who also had it rededicated, so now it's fully operational, albeit somewhat cobwebby inside.

There is to be a wedding there shortly, and Obbe is agog. 'Can't you stay until after the event?' I pleaded with B. as we wire-brushed the rusty ecclesiastical lamp-hangings and coated them with black paint ready for the great day. But alas it could not be arranged. She had business back in that other world, and so it comes about that I'm sitting here alone this morning waiting for the arrival of the wedding guests from far and wide, with the great house open to the public and the bedroom glowing upstairs with a log fire for the bride to change before.

Brushed, polished, whitened on its surrounds as though wearing a new pair of tennis shoes inside, those lamp brackets are still swinging gently from the trimming of the two Tilley lamps. The altar and lectern is spruced with wax polish and there is but one filmy cobweb high in the west window which caught the final shafts of sun yesterday eve ... so that none had had the heart to remove the miracle. I tell you, St Columba too, is agog.

So now, fresh from the mists of a mirror-calm Sound, Penelope, bride-to-be, disembarks from her longboat like some blonde Viking princess and leaps across the rocks to the north of the bay, followed close by the Lord Bishop of

Argyll and the Isles carrying robes, mitre and portable crook in a battered suitcase. Close on his heels comes the Reverend Philip B. from Obbe, for it is he who is to conduct the ceremony, and who is this but the bride's mother and father coming hot-foot across the grass . . . and the first glint of sunshine blesses the isle as the clock shows ten . . .

Into the house she goes with her retinue and up to the large room where the fire is welcoming, and preparations begin for that alchemy which will transform the chrysalis into that gossamer butterfly shortly to emerge.

But hasten! Already across the Sound comes the distant throb of another boat, echoing over the water which seems to be holding its breath in suspense, as though catching something of the magic. How long is it truly, St Columba, since you last held your arms above the heads of two about to become one – here on this isle?

So forty or so wedding guests, standing packed tight in the long green ferryboat from Uist, sweep into the bay and gaze apprehensively shorewards. How are they to land, with but one small rowing boat in tow? Why . . . *Lugworm* of course! So *Obbe-Wobble* is hastily cast into the water and I row out in her, slip *Lugworm*'s mooring and speed to the relieved guests.

'Twelve,' I shout. 'Not one more, lest Neptune see his opportunity and baptise the lot of us! Twelve only at a time can we take.'

Mothers and aunts, uncles and clergymen, cousins and friends totter, skid and fall pell-mell into the cockpit. And who's this . . . a kilted piper, complete with chanter and drones, come to send the couple speeding on a blast of joyous Highland air . . . so we beach, and a surge of swell lifts *Lugworm* far up the sand then recedes, so that the first to disembark, morning-suited and toppered, thinking to step dryfoot gets the laughing edge of the following wave that fills the polished shoes with saltwater and grit! It's piggy-backs for the remainder then, and only one camera taken as sacrifice for a safe landing by Old Neptune – and that returned good-naturedly, albeit somewhat soppy.

And now we are all ashore and drifting up to the chapel, crowding to the back like hushed sheep as though the altar had the mumps . . . and waiting. We have a tape recorder with potted organ and the acoustics in here are very good so that if you close your eyes ... why, you might be in Paul's so echoing is the music ... and now, silence ...

Silence, through which comes breathing the gentle hiss of the two Tilley lamps swinging there above us in the brackets.

From outside comes the deep sighing of the sea down there on the beach, and the far distant crying of a plover. A wide-eyed cow, against the far fence, lifts her head and ... *MMOOOOOOO!*

Silence.

Inside here it is so still that the gold candles atop the two altar posts send their yellow flames in perfect ovals roofward – twin glows that are echoed by the two plain white candles one either side the crucifix above the lace altar cloth ... and behind the altar in the window a bunch of purple island heather catches the light.

Whispering silence ...

A rustle! Through the door comes the goldlace glory, the mitred Bishop, who but two years since reintroduced this for-saken little chapel to Christ. Now comes the Reverend in plain white surplice ... and here is the groom, bearded and looking VERY young in his immaculate morning coat, trembling per-haps just a little.

Silence. You could hear a pin drop on the thick coconut matting so hastily taken from the front room of the house ...

Another rustle. A gossamer Penelope enters, cocooned in cream, on the arm of her father in black tails, and a whisper-ing dies.

So to the first hymn :

> *Father, hear the prayer we offer:*
> *Not for ease that prayer shall be,*
> *But for strength, that we may ever*
> *Live our lives courageously ...*

and the taped organ, well-intentioned mindless thing, does not know that the congregation cannot sing in unison at that pace, and outstrips them ... but we begin to get the hang of it by the Offertory and the second hymn; *Come down, O Love Divine* produces a full-blooded confidence by the last verse.

A little later, while Penelope secretly fingers the ring on her finger, her clergyman-uncle gives a short address which might well be remembered by all on earth who take that vow:

'In that part of Africa where my wife and I have lived and worked for forty years,' he tells the now betrothed couple, 'the villages are simply clusters of what are called *rondavels* – straw huts – and outside they all look the same, but if you go into them, you will find there are two different kinds. One has a central pole, the other has none. The one which has the central pole looks stronger: it has something you can see holding up the roof. But the people don't like it because that central pole gets in the way – it takes up too much room!

'You know, such a dwelling might symbolise a state of marriage where one person tries to be dominant – whether it's the man or the woman is no odds. If one tries to be dominant, that one gets in the way of a mutual understanding . . . gets in the way of true love.

'Now, in the other type of hut you'll find there isn't a central pole at all. But if you were to look up, you'd find that instead of just a cluster of rafters holding the roof up, there are two main ones, tied together with a little ring of cord. The local people will relate to you a parable which, in wisdom, they hand down from one generation to another. They say that the two rafters which are tied together represent husband and wife – and all the others represent the family.

'Man and wife are joined by that tie.

'If that tie breaks, the roof collapses.

'The home collapses.

'The tie is there to take the strain. A very considerable strain, time and time again. That is what it is there for.

'So,' he continues, 'we might remember the final words of the hymn we sung right at the beginning of this service . . .

> *Be our strength in hours of weakness*
> *In our wanderings, be our Guide,*
> *Through endeavour, failure, danger,*
> *Father, be Thou at our side.*

We all think a bit, about that . . .

Then the Bishop conducts a shortened Communion Service, and we sing *The Lord's my Shepherd*.

The bride takes her husband's arm and, to the strains of the Wedding March, walks out of the chapel to where the piper, ready at the door, takes up the joy and sounds it out across the isle and across the breathlessly still water, and the echo comes back to us from the old house walls, and the sheep and the cows, the lambs and the calves and a thousand birds are alerted and stop in their tracks or take to the wing . . .

And the couple, with two young bridesmaids holding the long veil clear of the thistles and the cowpats, walk to the echoing pipes down the hill to the house . . .

But what's afoot? The top-hatted father of the bride looks concerned. 'Where's the small boat that's to take the bridal party back to Obbe ahead of the guests?' he asks. No sign.

To *Lugworm* then!

Piggy-backs again with the piper landing on his bottom, kilt, sporran and bagpipes flying in a flurry of legs down into the cockpit, and the bride and groom with skirts and veil, trousers and shoes high as possible staggering through the surf to tumble aspluther into the boat, and Goodness! Here we all are again in *Lugworm*, her four horsepower manfully gasping at full throttle and bow sunk deep beneath the load of ten adults so that there's scarce freeboard at the scupper-holes . . . but the Piper regardless stands straight as a fathom of pumpwater at her stern, one precautionary arm around the mizzen mast, and plays us out of the bay and across the Sound to Obbe where the crowd is collecting. Three seals, their great eyes wide and liquid as the bride's own, come swimming in company, lured by the strange, haunting notes of the pipes which echo off the distant flanks of Roneval.

On the way back, the ferryboat, be-Bishopped, reverential and aglow with a job well and truly done, reciprocates in a festivity of waving . . . 'See you at the reception . . . See you at Strond . . .' come the cries . . . ships that pass.

So back to the benumbed and suddenly empty isle, and up to the chapel where the two exhausted Tilley lamps are at their last gasp, and the candles are snuffed . . . and St Columba all but snoozing again.

But there's something strangely different . . . Something in the air . . .

I have it.

St Columba is chuckling in his sleep!

Chapter Seven

Tir-an-Og

Ensay House
September 1975

My dear Katie and Nicky,

A whole summer now have I been on this enchanted isle, and all too few letters have I penned to my favourite two young beauties. But I ask you to believe (which you won't) that despite this fact you have both been often in my thoughts.

Shortly I shall have to leave the isles, for autumn is ap-proaching. But while I'm still here I must tell you of some more things which *Lugworm* and I have learned. To begin with, we have arranged for a young friend, Simon, of about your age Katie, to come across as often as possible in the farm boat during the winter with meat and milk for Grabbersnatch (who sends her love). Simon is deaf, but of course on that account he sees and feels very much more than you or I, so I am happy for Grabbers for I know I can trust him.

The next thing I must tell you is that I have discovered that these islands, so far up here off the west coast of Scotland, are really and truly enchanted – for they have the power to keep one young for ever! The ancient Gaels, who lived in these parts before even the Norsemen came sailing down in their ships from Scandinavia, knew this. They called the islands 'Tir-an-Og', which means the Land of Youth.

You may ask how did they discover this magic spell which haunts the round green hillocks in the sea, and the secret white sandy coves, and the hidden sea-echoing kelp-dark grot-toes? Why, it's quite easy: they lived here, as I am doing!

131

Before you know it the spell is working quietly, creeping into the very marrow of your bones, suffusing your brainbox, spilling out of your ears and tripping you headlong whenever you try, bemusedly, to cling on to 'respectability' and comfortable conventions! Goodness me! You see what I mean? Quite mad one becomes when the magic is fermenting ... and believe me, it's bubbling up this night!

I think it's the sky really that triggers it all off. True, you can go out and look at the sky wherever you are and it's always beautiful; even in an odd sort of way when it's raining ... particularly in Cornwall where you can get out to the cliffs and almost become part of it with the wind blowing through you and taking something of you with it to freedom. But here! Oh, HERE the sky is entirely different, due I suppose to its having to change its nature simply by being so very close to heaven.

Can you understand what I mean? It is no longer just the sky up there ... it is an immensity beyond you that speaks of something so much greater – infinitely distant yet all about and showing itself in all things – just obtainable, half-sensed, yet really known deep down with certainty, because what we are *now* is born from this strange and seemingly far-off *Greatness*. It is not just *there* and *there*, but *here* and *here* as well – and everywhere and in everything, so that it is all One.

Wise men of old, in a very ancient language called Sanscrit, sometimes referred to the joy of this half-sensed *One-ness* by an odd name. They called it *Ishwara*. Perhaps we today might call it God, but the tragedy is that people who really do not possess the capacity have diminished this joy into a mere ritual involving ideas of guilt, and suffering, which are nourished in solemn dark buildings containing effigies and glittering jewels on altars ... and it's all very confusing so infinitely far is it, and so little has any of it to do with Ishwara, which we might call God.

If you really want to glimpse the face of Ishwara, and you happen to be lucky enough to be the friend of a boat like *Lugworm* ... then you have but to hoist her sails and hear them catch the song of the wind which sweeps across these waters – and let her glide out of the bay in front of this rambling old mansion on this magic island. Before you can even start singing, Ishwara is here with you in *Lugworm* and in the sea and the mountains all about, but most of all in the wind and the sky!

Sometimes, very rarely, Ishwara can be felt actually in what we call *ourselves*. Then EVERYTHING changes completely!

It happened yesterday evening. *Lugworm* and I, together with *Obbe-Wobble*, whom you will remember was born of driftwood on the beach, were nosing quietly up north of our island toward a mountain over the sea-horizon called Taobh Deas. We were bound there because a great Golden Eagle has its eyrie somewhere on the slopes and all three of us very much wanted the bird to catch sight of us and know we are here.

The sun was an enormous red ball that seemed to float in an amber mist where the horizon should have been, and gradually, from out of the north, came slowly rolling another ocean of luminous cloud. We all watched, so majestically did that greater sea-mist which overlaid the real sea move in from over the edge of the world. Then a wonderfully unexpected thing took place.

As though awakened from sleep, the front edge of that sea-cloud opened its eyes with shock at feeling the hard shoulders of Taransay and Lewis (both of which are islands) and it caught fire and leapt . . . high, high into the vault of the sky in a curtain of miraculous flame! It was immense – stretching from the beginnings to the ends of space – and the whole edge of the world glowed in the light from that towering cliff of fire that clawed at Heaven itself! This tiny world went quiet in awe, and flushed gold at the majesty of it . . . and that is the moment when a thrilling madness came over everything – *Lugworm, Obbe-Wobble*, the mountains, the islands, the sea and sky and me.

Lugworm suddenly threw her anchor overboard and down it plunged blowing bubbles through fathoms of wine-dark laughing water. Then she furled her sails, for the wind was holding her breath quite still, and I saw we were in a small bay under the mountain where the eagle lives. Straight into that cool, plum-green water I plunged (for one never wears any clothes on enchanted islands) and swam to the sands which were still embracing the noonday warmth of sun. Oh, Katie and Nicky ... will YOU ever clamber from a cool, plum-green sea and run naked along the warm sands, up through great dunes, over the grassy tops of them, and then roll over and over and over in the warm heather-scented grass? I did, then I ran on again to the slopes of the mountain and finally stood straight and looked at the sky above it's peak and sang, loud as I could ... loud as is possible for such a mite thing in this immense and wonderful world, for of course I had to sing for *Lugworm* and *Obbe-Wobble* and for that mountain and the sea and sky, all of whom so deeply wanted to share the magic too ...

... For, you see, only I was articulate

... only I have a mind

... only I was aware

... and suddenly I understood what I have never understood before: that it was not I who was exulting in the mountains, and the sea and sky and islands – it was the mountains, and sea, and sky and the islands which were exulting through me!

This was the moment when I glimpsed the face of Ishwara, in the mirror of space.

A strange madness, but one which I very much hope you will share. Of course you don't actually have to live on an enchanted island to find the key – because, as I've tried to show, Ishwara is everywhere. Indeed, some people of much greater perception than I have discovered this in the most unlikly places ... but for such as me, islands do help!

So perhaps you will understand why *Lugworm* and I will always remember Tir-an-Og. *Obbe-Wobble* will not need to remember for she is staying here (which is only right, for she was born here). She is staying with Simon, who is already a good swimmer, and rows her beautifully.

Tonight, as I write this in front of the great log fire glowing here in the stove, the yellow beam of my oil lamp is falling on yet another face of Ishwara – sheets of glittering rain borne by a roaring gale that shrieks round the eaves of the old house and moans on out high over *Lugworm* and across the blackness of the Sound. We could be lonely if we did not know that there are people and animals and 'things' with whom we can share this happiness.

Perhaps that is how – in us – Ishwara grows?

My love,
Ken